The *Range Riders* cover captures the essence of the Western pulp magazine as does the fiction that it represented. The slap-leather moment, a moment of high tension, a life-and-death moment. Similarly, the Range Riders stories reflected the same circumstances, with verisimilitude, sometimes seeming to represent circumstances of the 'real' West.

The action was slap-leather, slam-bang: "With a single whipping motion Steeve Reese drew his .38 and fired" and the action was always set against a vivid, Western backdrop: "Pushing up the great valley, hemmed in by purple-red cliffs and grassed by irrigation, Reese took it all in." In the hands of a skilled writer the mythic West was never victimized by the realities of Western geography or history. Tom Curry wrote these words (*Range Riders Western*, Summer '43: "Colorado Blood") and several million others over a long career in the pulps, al of which were drawn from a formula:

> "The general theme must be that the hero, being young, handsome, strong, personable, and being endowed with great moral courage and character, as well as being an expert shot, fist-fighter, cowpuncher and rider, must, in willingly facing the most hazardous missions, track down, confront and defeat the villain in violent physical combat...And like all romantic adventure stories, these yarns must have a happy ending, as far as the hero is concerned, that is."
>
> – Tom Curry

While the (three) Range Riders adhered to the Western formula there were some things to bother, among which was the fact that they are variously described as 'avengers' and cattle detectives; labels which ring familiar to the resumes of some real Western badmen.

The lead Range Rider, Steeve Reese's background is uncomfortably similar to that of Tom Horn. Horn was an ex-Pinkerton hired by the Wyoming Stock-Growers Association in their range fights with Wyoming sheepmen. It was understood by the WSGA that he was nothing but a hired assassin and Horn was eventually hung for killing a fourteen-year old boy.

Ranger Rider Reese was an ex-St. Louis police lieutenant hired as a field agent by the Cattlemen's Protective Association. In one encounter ("Boothill or Bust," *Range Riders Western*, Spring 1943) Reese is referred to as "the CPA regulator." Regulators were nothing more than vigilantes the likes of real-life Western badman Clay Allison.

Fortunately Reese's CPA was solidly on the side of law and order and the Range Riders yarns proved to be satisfying cowboy fiction: fiction with enough variation in authorship to keep the series interesting. Of the many who wrote for this series my favorite is C. William Harrison. Harrison had the ability to create a little apprehension in the reader's mind as he did in the following scene where Steeve Reese has just passed through the swinging doors of a frontier bar:

> "The solitaire player had forgotten his cards and was watching Reese narrowly. The man on the opposite side of the room was stirring out of his feigned sleep, but he didn't pull his hands out from under the table. A gun, drawn and ready, was resting in his lap, faintly outlined by the spill of gray light through the dusty window."

> – "Boothill or Bust," Spring 1943.

The Pulp Western

A Popular History of the
Western Fiction Magazine in America

by John A. Dinan

The Pulp Western

A Popular History of the
Western Fiction Magazine in America

by John A. Dinan

BearManor Media
2003

The Pulp Western:
A Popular History of the Western Fiction Magazine in America
© 2003 by John A. Dinan. All rights reserved.

For information, address:

BearManor Media
P. O. Box 750
Boalsburg, PA 16827

bearmanormedia.com

Cover design by John Teehan
Typesetting and layout by John Teehan

Published in the USA by BearManor Media
ISBN—1-59393-003-8

To Clint Scott, for all his time and effort

To the Western Writers of America,
for all the help from its members,
and for all those pulp Western yarns.

Table of Contents

The Cover .... inset

Foreword i

In The Beginning—The Dime Novels 1

The Pulp Western 7

The Romance Western 33

The Hero Western 37

Further Variations 51

The Pulp Western Story 57

Other Writing Techniques 69

The Men Behind the Masks—The Editors 73

Hacking Them Out By the Dozens — The Writers 81

To "B" Or Not To "B"—the Pulps & the Movies 123

Beneath a Pastel Sun—The Artists 129

The End To the Trail—The Demise of the Pulp Fiction 135

Afterword 143

Bibliography 147

Index 151

Foreword

The working cowboy would never be found in great abundance in the pulp magazines, or in the dime novels, in hard- or soft-cover books, or something else. A man for all seasons, the cowboy of fiction survives because of the genius of first-rate authors like James Fenimore Cooper and such modern masters of the art as Fred Glidden (Luke Short) and Ernest Haycox, and in spite of the works of hacks like Edward Judson (Ned Buntline). This book covers a generation, the pulp era of the 1920's, '30's, and '40's of pulp fictioneers who cranked out millions, perhaps even hundreds of millions, or words for the several hundred western pulp magazines then active. I have also tried to produce some sense of continuity in the development of a genre by providing a short history of the origins of Western American fiction, plus a brief commentary on the genre's evolution into the paperback era.

During this 25-year period, the pulps published Western fiction in phenomenal abundance, reflecting the public's desire of escapist reading. There has been, perhaps, no greater amount of written material produced in such a short time on a given theme, before or since. The following list of magazines devoted exclusively to Western fiction does not include the early generation fiction pulps, some of which produced excellent Western stories, but only those periodicals devoted primarily to the Western theme.

Ace High Magazine
Ace High Novels
Ace High Western Stories
Ace Western
Action Packed Western

Best Western Magazine
Best Western Novels
Big Book Western Magazine
Big Chief Western
Blazing Western

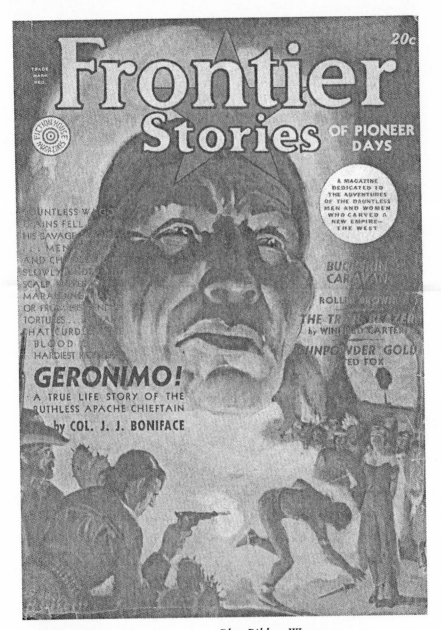

Action Stories
All American Western
All Novel Western
All Story Western
All Western Magazine
Complete Cowboy Novel
Complete Northwest Novel

Blue Ribbon Western
Buck Jones Western Stories
Bullseye Western
Candid Western
Complete Cowboy Magazine
Complete Cowboy – Wild West Stories
Complete Novel Western

Complete Western –
  Book Magazine
Cowboy Movie Thrillers
Cowboy Short Stories
Crack Shot Western
Double Action Western
Exciting Western
Far West Illustrated
Fifteen Range Romances
Fighting Western
44 Western
Frontier Stories
Golden West Magazine
Greater Western Magazine
Gunsmoke Western
Indian Stories
Leading Western
Lone Star Ranger
Mammoth Western Quarterly
Maverick Magazine
Movie Western
Nickel Western
Northwest Stories
Old West
Pete Rice Magazine
Pioneer Western
Popular Western
Quick Trigger Western Novels
Ranch Romances
Rangeland Stories
Rapid Fire Western Stories
Real West
Real Western Mystery Novels
Real Western Stories
Red Star Western
The Rio Kid Western
Romance Range
Romance Western
Romantic Round-up
Romantic Western Novel
  Magazine
Six Gun Western
Speed Western
Star Western Magazine

Complete Western –
  Love Novelettes
Cowboy Romances
Cowboy Stories
Dime Western Magazine
Dynamic Western
Famous Western Magazine
Far West Stories
Fifteen Western Range Romances
Five Western Novels
The Frontier
Giant Western
Golden West Romances
Gun Swift Western
Hopalong Cassidy Western Magazine
Lariat Story Magazine
The Lone Ranger
Luke Short's Western
Masked Rider Western Magazine
Max Brand Western Magazine
New Western Magazine
Northwest Romances
Outlaws of the West
Pecos Kid Western
Pete Rice Western Adventures
Pocket Western Magazine
Posse
Ranch Love Stories
Rangeland Love Story Magazine
Rangeland Sweethearts
Real Northwest Magazine
Real Western Magazine
Real Western Romances
Red Seal Western
Riders of the Range
Rodeo Romances
Romance Roundup
Romantic Range
Romantic West Annual
Silver Buck Western
Smashing Western
Spicy Western
Stirring Detective and Western
  Stories

Story Western Magazine
Sure Fire Western
Texas Rangers
Three Western Novels Magazine
Thrilling Western
Top Westerns
Tops in Western Stories
Treasury of Great Western Stories
Triple X Western
True Western and Far West
Two Gun Stories

Super Western
Ten Story Western Magazine
Texas Western
Thrilling Ranch Stories
Top Notch Westerns
Top Western Fiction Annual
Tops in Westerns
Triple Western
True Western Adventures
True Western Stories
Two Gun Western

Two Gun Western Novels
Two Gun Western Stories
Two Western Romances
Wagon Train
Walt Coburn's Western
West Magazine
Western Ace High Stories
Western Action
Western Action Thrillers
Western Adventures
Western Dime Novel
Western Fiction Magazine
Western Love Romances
Western Love Story
Western Magazine
Western Novel Magazine
Western Novelettes
Western Raider
Western Rangers
Western Romance Anthology
Western Round-up
Western Tales
Western Winners
Wild Bill Hickock Western
   (never printed)
Wild West Stories & Complete
   Novel Magazine
Wild Western Novels

Two Gun Western Action Books
Two Western Books
Variety Western
Walt Coburn's Action Novels
The West
West Weekly
Western Aces
Western Action Novels
Western Action Two Books
Western Book
Western Fiction
Western Love Magazine
Western Love Stories
Western Love Story Magazine
Western Novel and Short Stories
Western Novel of the Month
Western Outlaws
The Western Ranger Stories
Western Rodeo Romances
Western Romances
Western Supernovel Magazine
Western Trails
Western Yarns
Wild West Stories

Wild West Weekly

Zane Grey's Western Story Magazine

The above enumeration includes some 165 titles, yet there may be some undiscovered titles out there.

Western fiction in general, and Western pulp fiction in particular, was and is today disdained by devotees of the early science-fiction pulps, the hero pulps, the detective pulps, and even horror pulp addicts. In spite of its generally bad reputation, (Ron Goulart in *Cheap Thrills* relegates pulp Westerns to "the bottom of the pulp barrel"), the Western pulp story was printed, distributed, and presumably read in greater numbers than any other popular literature. The literacy or social significant of the Western pulp is not to be found in a type of plot, a style of writing, or even a "message", there were few innovations ever made in the basic Western formula. Instead, the significance of the Western pulp magazine clearly lies in the number of publications produced and the obvious size of the public appetite for this material. Its evident popularity with generations of American readers must surely represent a widespread belief in and hope for the myth of Western frontier America, where men and women could begin their lives anew, where "men were men" and "women were women," where individualist could operate free of restrictions from society, where no man need fear anything but his own fear. This was the vision of the pulp Western.

In the Beginning— The Dime Novels

ENVOI

Take up the long neglected pen,
Redeem its valiant steel from rust
And write these magic words again:
"Another redskin bit the dust!"
From *Dime Novels*, Edmund Pearson

"The Street and Smith enterprises like the *Buffalo Bill* stories, the *Log Cabin Library*, the *Jesse James* stories, the *Tip-Top Weekly* and the *Red, White and Blue Library* together with Frank Tousey publications like the *Boy's Story Library*, *Frank Munsey's Weekly*, and the *New York Detective Library*, the *Pluck and Luck* stories and *Wild West Weekly*—the cheap series widening downward from the 1890's into the twentieth century almost baffle enumeration—lead straight from the Beadle publications to the Westerns of the present day"
— *Virgin Land*, Henry Naish Smith

"First and foremost, the dime novel was big business. Never before or since has book publishing held a larger share of the gross national product"
— *Eight Dime Novels*, E.F. Bleiler

1

To understand the Western pulp magazines, we must go back to the last quarter of the nineteenth century. During the period from 1878, when the adventures of the Diamond Dicks first appeared in *New York Weekly*, to the first appearance of *Young Wild West* just after the turn of the century, the American Western frontier was moving rapidly toward the Pacific Ocean, and constantly outstripping the civilizing influences that followed reluctantly. Communication on the frontier was largely word-of-mouth, despite such innovations as telegraph and telephone; when an Eastern reporter would finally show up at the site of some newsworthy event, chances were that the event itself was long since passed. By this time, local witnesses had embellished their observations or hearsay beyond any semblance of reality. In some cases, as with Buffalo Bill, this was done deliberately by promoters. The art of ballyhoo may not have been invented by dime-novel writers, but they certainly raised it to new heights.

It is most difficult to sort fact from fancy when trying to understand the West of this period. Even a first-rate nonfiction account such as Francis Parkman's *The Oregon Trail* is suspect since it represents the observations of one single man (an inexperienced Easterner at that), and often reflects an obviously patronizing attitude toward the Indian.

Perhaps the ultimate fiction lies in the fact that these "Westerns" did not concern themselves with the working cowboy. Defined in *The American Cowboy in Life and Legend* as "not a cattle baron or a Western gunslinger but simply a man who plies the crafts of the cattle ranch," the American cowboy was not to be found in popular Western fiction of either the dime novel of pulp era.

The dime novel Western, *Seth Jones* or, *Captives of the Frontier*, sold over 400,000 copies. Later dime novel Western stories reached similar readerships, and were perhaps the most widely read popular literature of their time (1860-1920). The best-selling dime novels were always the Westerns, whether they featured the fictional cowboy such as Young Wild West, the romanticized cowboy such as Buffalo Bill, or the first of the fictionalized anti-hero types, such as the Dalton Gang or the James Boys. The original dime novels were produced in a four-story factory in New York by the firm of Beadle and Adams the principals being Erastus Flavel Beadle, Editor Orville J. Victor, and Robert Adams. Victor played a vital role in shaping the writing styles, as well as setting the pace at which the writers worked. Western fiction was cranked out in some cases at thousands of (pre-typewriter) words an hour by "authors whose nearest acquaintance with the Great Plains was in White Plains, New York," according to Edmund Pearson, author of *Dime Novels*.

These "novels" often referred to derisively as "yellow backs," changed format, size, or title over the years, but could always be stuffed in a pocket or nailed to a privy wall.

One evening in Boston in 1884, Orville Victor was asked to comment on the genealogy of the dime novel hero, to which he replied that the Beadle Western hero followed Cooper's tales (the five Leather stocking stories) which suggested him. Today, the leather stocking and dime novel prose looks extremely stilted, if not downright silly. A potboiler formula story is readable if written in the idiom of the day, but as it ages, it becomes no more than a parody of itself.

Two of the more interesting Western dime novel characters were Young Wild West, who made his first appearance in a dime novel of the same name in 1902 and Deadwood Dick, who first appeared in the first issue of Beadle's Pocket Library in 1884.

Deadwood Dick was the rootin'-tootin', ridin', shootin', and romancin' type of cowboy, while Young Wild West, the prototype for pulp super heroes to follow, was a master hand with both rifle and revolver, had a mysterious supply of gold coins, and a coterie of associates, all in search of adventure. Above all, Young Wild West and his crew possessed a solid sense of right and wrong, all of which was sufficient to carry the boys over 644 stories and many later reprints. Street and Smith's Buffalo Bill Series ran 591 issues, from 1901 to 1912, and the *New Buffalo Bill Weekly* picked up from there, continuing through 1917. The last eight issues of the magazine were then re-titled as *Western Story Library*. The *New Buffalo Bill Weekly/Western Story Library* became *Western Story Magazine* with Volume 7, No. 9, dated August 9, 1919. This magazine would eventually become the cream of the Western pulp magazines.

Ted Strong, cowboy hero property of Street and Smith, didn't appeal as much to the dime novel readers, since his exploits were too closely focused about ranch and range life. Strong, a sergeant with Col. Roosevelt's Rough Riders in the Spanish-American War, had inherited a cattle range in the Black Hills of Dakota. It was here that Strong would fight cattle rustlers, the Sioux, and unsuccessfully compete with Young Wild West for the dime novel market. *Rough Rider Weekly* (the dime novel that featured Strong) lasted a mere 175 issues.

The later dime novels included the so-called biography type (fictionalized exploits of prominent Western characters such as Billy the Kid), fiction based on a shaky nonfiction framework; no one did these better than Ned Buntline.

The "King of the Dime Novels," Buntline whose real name was Edward Zane Carroll Judson, took his pseudonym from the rope at the bottom of a square sail. He led a flamboyant life as a sailor, prohibitionist (who delivered few of his temperance lectures in a state of sobriety), soldier, writer, itinerant con man, and troublemaker, then became most famous for his Buffalo Bill dime novels. Perhaps Buntline's greatest significance is the role he played as the link between J. Fenimore Cooper (whom he had read as a boy) and the Western pulp story. If not the originator of the mass-produced Western fiction story, Buntline was certainly almost solely responsible for the popular success of Western fiction over the last quarter of the nineteenth century. He never considered his abysmal lack of knowledge of things Western as anything but a minor obstacle, thereby setting a precedent that the other dime novel fictioneers would soon imitate. Gilbert Patten, (Frank Merriwell's "father") once wrote dime-novel Westerns under the name Wyoming Bill, having "earned" this curious *nom de plume* by having once been a passenger on a train that passed through Wyoming.

Outside of the insular world of the dime novel, a singular event in Western fiction was taking place in the first decade of the twentieth. Western fiction was taking place in the first decade of the twentieth century – the publication of the first bestselling cowboy story, *The Virginian*, by Owen Wister. *The Virginian* gave us believable dialogue (in comparison to its competitors; by today's standards, it seems stiff and stilted), and the first tough-but-cool cowboy ("When you call me that, smile!"). Frank Gruber maintained that *The Virginian* took the Western out of the woodshed and put it in the parlor. In any event, *The Virginian* provided a prototype cowboy that is still being imitated in fiction today.

The dime novels didn't die out right away, but the bulk of the dime novels surviving into the 1920's were reprints of older publications. Overburdened by juvenile plotting and a prose style that had seen its day come and go, the end of the dime novels was in sight, a fact that was now being recognized by their publishers.

While the early Western pulp magazines showed no significant improvements initially (after all, they were being written by the same men and being produced by the same publishing houses that produced the dime novels), with time and new talent we would see less of, "I'm called Buffalo Billy… Then if you know me you will understand that though I am but a boy I won't let you walk away with my claim," and more of, "Suddenly the dull animal flashed into life. He tore the pistol from the numbed grip, and with one savage leap swung the brassbound butt against the temple of the Mexican. The blow sounded hollow. The blue bruise upon his temple became diffused with blood."

These were the sights and sounds of the pulp Western.

"Most real-life cowboys were just that—boys between 18 and 25, unwilling to stay at home with pasture and plow, they became hired hands on horseback. Most did not own their own horses and few rose above their humble station"

– William Savage,
Cowboy Life: Reconstructing an American Myth

"The fight to launch a new pulp and keep an old one going is a never-ending one"

– Harold Hersey, *Pulpweed Editor*

> "In one sense the Western formula is far easier to define than that of the detective story, for when we see a couple of characters dressed in ten-gallon hats and riding horses, we know we are in a Western"
>
> – *The Six-Gun Mystique*, John G. Cawelti

The Pulp Western

THE PULP WESTERN

The pulp pedigree is difficult to establish. The early general fiction pulps such as *Popular* and *Argosy* merged, combined, and dissolved in almost mitotic fashion. For example, Frank Munsey incorporated *The Live Wire* into *The Scrap Book* in 1908, in 1912, *The Cavalier* was absorbed by *The Scrap Book*, but in 1914 *The Scrap Book* was taken out of this combination and combined with *All-Story Weekly* (now called *All-Story Cavalier Weekly*) and so forth. This kind of evolution would continue into the comic books. *Adventure*, which had run some historical-type Western fiction in its pulp years, would later evolve into *Adventure Comics*, which in turn would later become *Action Comics* and *Detective Comics*.

As we have seen with the dime novel, *The Buffalo Bill Weekly* evolved into *The New Buffalo Bill Weekly* (Featuring reprints of the Buffalo Bill Stories), then became *The New Buffalo Bill Weekly/Western Story Library*, and finally *Western Story Magazine*. The roots of the Western pulp magazines were firmly planted in the dime novels, just as the pulp magazines themselves later evolved simultaneously into comic books and paperbacks.

Western Story Magazine was the prototype all-Western pulp magazine, running for thirty years with quality Western yarns by such giants of the field as Frederick Faust ("Max Brand") and Fred Glidden.

All of this combining and dissolving of titles was done to avoid issuing new titles (which would result in higher postal rates), and to kill off magazines with declining circulations without eliminating the possibility of someday bringing them back.

The bulk of Western pulp fiction was written by males for males. The fictional pulp cowboy had no family life and no permanent relationships. The so-called "romance Westerns" was the exception to the rule. While they had almost an all-female readership, Street and Smith pulp editor Daisy Bacon informs me that 55% of these stories were written by men. When the cowboy of the pulps came to what Falke has called "the end of the trail" (marriage and domesticated family life), he would find his survival here (while the pulp cowboy was mostly off the newsstands by the late 1940s and early '50s, the romance Western would hang on for another decade).

The general fiction pulp magazines of the early 1920s continued to produce occasional Westerns. These included Munsey's *Argosy*, Ridgway's *Adventure*, Street and Smith's *Popular*, Doubleday's *Short Stories*, and McCall's *Blue Book*, whose enormous combined circulations provided some of the highest payment levels among the pulps and whose editorial policies encompassed fine action adventure writing of all kinds.

However, the trend was clearly toward the all-Western story pulp. Soon a straight diet of Western fiction would become available in the form of short stories (under 10,000 words), novelettes (10,000-60,000 words), and novels (60,000 words plus), not to mention an endless variety of special columns and features. The big-gun Western fictioneers like Faust and H. Bedford-Jones generally worked at novel length, their stories being serialized over four to six issues of the more frequently published magazines. The latter war years would see a publication impatient with serials, but during their heyday, they provided the greatest financial return possible to the pulp writer.

The early all-Western pulp magazines (with origins in the 1920s) include *West* and *Frontier* (Doubleday), *Cowboy Stories, Ace High, Ranch Romances*, and *Western Adventures* (Clayton), *Triple X Western* (Fawcett), *Lariet*, and *North West Stories* (Fiction House).

The pulp magazines produced, on occasion, some durable fiction, although many were downright terrible. In a recent interview, Harry Sinclair Drago (whose stories date back to the 1920's) ranked *Argosy, Popular, Western Story*, and *Short Stories* as the best publishers of Western fiction, while Wayne D. Overholser (a postwar paperback Western writer for Dell and Ballantine) ranks *Dime Western, Ten Story Western,* and *Ranch Romances* as the best Western pulp magazines. One thing common to all of these publications, and possibly a reason for their high ranking by writers, is longevity, which translates into durable markets for the Western fictioneers.

Western Story was perhaps the most popular of the Western pulps with readers of the day. In addition to being the first Western pulp magazine (having been converted from dime-novel format in 1919), it produced consistently high quality fiction by such writers as William Colt McDonald,

Fred Glidden (Luke Short), Hugh Cave, Walt Coburn, Frederick Faust (Max Brand, Evan Evans, etc.), and W.C. Tuttle. Each of these men was not only a first-rate storyteller, but had had some experience with the American West on a first-hand basis. Cover and interior artwork were a large part of the pulp mystique, and *Western Story's* Gerry Delano and Nick Eggenhofer two of the best artists. As with most of the Western fiction magazines, *Western Story* stressed consistent standards (in the poorer pulps, these became rigid formulas) of entertainment, with somewhat firm parameters within which its writers had to work. In its early years, *Western Story* ran 144 pages and carried one novel, two serials, three short stories, one fact-type article, and the following "departments":

MINER'S POTLATCH: "*Western Story Magazine* desires this department to be of real assistance to all who are interested in the practical side of mining."

THE ROUND UP: Letters to the editor column consisting mostly of rambling talk about Western subjects.

THE HOLLOW TREE: "Miss Helen Rivers, who conducts this department, will see to it that you make friends with other readers, though thousands of miles may separate you."

WHERE TO GO AND HOW TO GET THERE: Reader queries on Western geography.

MISSING: This "department" was a heartbreaker and included such pleas as "Homer – Please write to mamma at the old address in Raton. Am very anxious to hear from you, fir I have much to tell you." - Signed E.L.C., Raton, N.M.; "F.O.S., come home immediately. Emma is very ill. Write to Heartbroken Anna in care of this magazine."

The *Western Story* format provided something for everyone, including the lonely and the troubled; and proved to be one of the few Western pulp magazines with a readership that was willing or interested enough to sustain two-way communications.

While *Western Story* had an excellent stable of writers and artists, the single force that made it an enduring success was Frederick Faust, King of

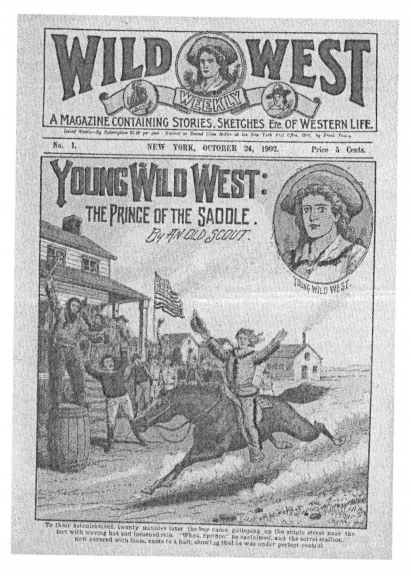

the Pulps, who could write the formula Western with a style that captured the Western addict's heart – and in the sufficient quantity to keep the presses rolling almost single-handedly. On at least two occasions, Faust would contribute three major stories to a single issue of *Western Story* (March 12, 1932, and again on April 2, 1932). Many of Faust's Western Story yarns remain in print today in paperback form (such was his being prolific that "new" Faust Westerns are still appearing in book form annually, resurrected from their pulp origins, in spite of his death nearly forty years ago).

Faust and others had "kid" stories that appeared on an on-and-off basis, *Western Story* had the Polka Dot Kid and the Montana Kid; other Western pulps had the Rio Kid, the Arizona Kid; and *Wild West Weekly*, one of *Western Stories'* biggest competitors, had a plethora; the Silver Kid, Kid Wolf, the Oklahoma Kid, the Sonoma Kid, and the Whistlin' Kid. *Wild West Weekly* has the distinction of being the only Western pulp magazine with a modern following. While collectors of super-heroes such as the Rio Kid or The Lone Ranger and collectors of the Spicy pulps might break your arm for an issue with E. Hoffmann Price yarn, these are not collectors interested in the Western story *per se*. The same holds for collectors of single authors such as Faust or Coburn. These people are more interested in the man than his work.

Wild West Weekly has, today, a hard core of devotees who collect and read these magazines with a passion born of a deep love of the Western yarn. The magazines are sold and traded via an underground that would do credit to the French Resistance Forces of World War II. It was from this underground fandom that I obtained the following remembrance of things past by Redd Boggs, editor and publisher of *Black Hat*, a newsletter "edited and published occasionally for CHAPS." It has been circulated among *Wild West Weekly* fans over the years, and is reprinted here in its entirety with Redd's permission. No one could tell the *Wild West Weekly* story better.

"I Remember Wild West Weekly"
by Red Boggs

"I've got over 400—and I'm looking for more"
– Clint Scott, collector of *Wild West Weekly* pulp magazines

How I became a 3W Fan

Like De Quincey and his opium, I first made acquaintance with Street and Smith's *Wild West Weekly* so long ago that I might have forgotten the date and the circumstances if it had been a trifling incident in my life. However, cardinal events are not to be forgotten, and by diligently searching my memory for fading recollections and the attic for the withering copy of the first issue of the magazine I ever bought, I can pin down the time and place almost exactly. It must have been the second or third day of August 1033, and I lived in Breckenridge, Minnesota at 299 Eighth Street South, in the house known in family annals as the Ross House. My introduction to *Wild West Weekly* arose in the following way.

In those days of boyhood, I was known to my schoolmates as "the kid who draws cowboy pictures." Drawing was my hobby and my passion in the early morning of my life, and all one summer when I was about ten or eleven I labored at creating an original sequel to Zane Grey's *Riders of the Purple Sage*, drawn in crude comic-strip form in the mode of Ed Wheelan's "Minute Movies." The reason why my friends and I should have imagined that I possessed any skill with a pencil cannot be inferred from the few scraps of drawings that have survived. I shuffle through them looking vainly for the smallest glint of talent.

Why I chose to draw cowboys instead of cheesecake is slightly more comprehensible. I was reading vastly of Zane Grey and the X Bar X Boys at the library; "cowboy movies" were my favorite Saturday entertainment and I was an eager fan of the short-lived comic strip called "Bronco Bill." Despite all these sources of inspiration, however, one day of the long summer vacation I found I required fresh inspiration. I decided that I needed to study the effects achieved by the illustrators of some western magazine that was filled with action drawings and stories I could try to illustrate.

Somehow, I managed to coax .20 from my mother, and waving aside her offer of an armored truck to convoy me, for of course, .20 was a fortune in those depression days. I sprinted down to Hoilichy's drugstore to select a suitable magazine from among the gaudy array on their newsstand. After thumbing all the Western magazines and jingling for dimes in my pocket meditatively, I finally chose a copy of Street and Smith's *Wild West Weekly*. As I blow the dust off it and glance through the August 5, 1933 issue today, trying to imagine how it must have looked on the news rack nearly three decades ago, I wonder why my eyes were attracted to it even momentarily. It is of little merit in displaying Wild West artwork. The front cover, by Kiemle, seems completely wooden and vague in outline. It is, indeed, unlike most pulp-magazine covers, very subdued in color, and arranged as a fuzzy vignette rather than as a full picture. The interiors by H.W. Scott are even less attractive than most pulp-magazine art, and I soon realized that Scott was an abomination comparable with Kremer, who had desecrated *Astounding* a few years later.

At any rate, *Wild West Weekly* happened to be the magazine I selected. I bought it—the price was only .15 not .20 and took it home to read. I sat in a chair on the front porch and read until it grew dark. As far as I can remember, I was not inspired to the drawing board that evening—or ever—by the magazine. Its effect was clearly opiate in character, as pleasant as De Quincey's laudanum and a good deal more habit-forming. After more than a quarter of a century, I can still remember parts of the stories I read that summer evening almost word for word. The lead novelette was "Smokey Clark—Trail Boss" by Ben Conlon, and it was backed by two other novelettes, "Tangled Herds" by Cleve Endicott, and "The Desert Phantom's Showdown" by Walker Tompkins, plus four shorts, "The Whistlin' Kid Climbs a Cliff" by Emery Jackson, "Some Sand, Ranger!" by Frank J. Litchfield, "The Thunder Bird at Gray Horse Mine" by Lee Harrington, and "The Sonora Kid—Not Guilty" by Allan R. Bosworth.

I enjoyed each of these stories outrageously, without exception. A few issues later, I began to grow more particular and even picky in attacking the weekly feast of reading. Two of my favorites in the first issue were the Conlon and the Harrington, and I will never forget how, in the latter yarn, the arch-villain known as the Thunder Bird escaped from Jail in Thunderbolt City during a wild rainstorm, leaving a taunting note weighted under a bar he had hacked off with a smuggled blade. "Gone on a gray Horse!" Both these stories were skillfully written; reading them over today for purposes of writing this scholarly dissertation, I find them superior examples of pulp-magazine art.

Best of all the stories in that August 5, 1933 issue was "The Desert Phantom's Showdown" by Walker Tompkins. This was the last story in a series of six yarns, but it was complete in itself, and capable of being enjoyed in splendid isolation, which I proceeded to do. It built up to a whacking climax, and the punch line, the final line of the story and the whole series, was "The courthouse clock was striking twelve." This yarn, colored with all the glories of the first impressions of a new delight, probably stands as my all-time favorite story from *Wild West Weekly*. One bumps into a "Desert Phantom" or a "Skylark of Space" only once in a lifetime, but the half-conscious aim of later reading is to discover another story in the same genre or by the same author that will produce as much pleasure. No story ever does, of course, and so there is always that little touch of sadness in the career of any fan.

On page 144, the last page of the issue, there was a large house and headed "Comin' Next Week!" which heralded the feature stories for the

August 12 issue. The cover story was to be "Dead Man's Trail" by Samuel H. Nickels, blurbed as the latest adventures of "Hungry and Rusty, them two fightin' Rangers." For some reason I proved particularly susceptible to the allure of the Texas Rangers, and I soon decided that I must buy one more issue of the magazine in order to read this story. Of course, I was already a slave to the habit and didn't realize it as yet.

Dated the Saturday of each week, *Wild West Weekly*, like the *Saturday Evening Post*, actually hit the newsstands in midweek. For several weeks, I bought the magazine each Thursday, which was the day of the week I had bought the first issue. Later, I discovered that the magazine appeared on the stands on Wednesday, and sometimes on Tuesday. Usually I bought my copy on Wednesday.

I read every issue of the magazine for exactly three months, but at the end of October 1933, with the darkest winter of the depression closing in, I couldn't even promote .15 a week for magazines any longer. I started to buy *Wild West Weekly* again in mid-January 1934, and thereafter bought it regularly for three years. By that time, I had begun to read *Astounding* regularly, and my interest in science fiction had long since begun to out blaze my enthusiasm for westerns. I kept buying *WWW* for old time's sake, and even after I ceased to read the magazine regularly, I occasionally bought copies of had them give to me, and so was able to follow its later career, which lasted another six years, almost seven.

THE GOLDEN YEARS, 1927-1939

In an earlier article on *Wild West Weekly*, which appeared in *Grue #29*, published by Dean A. Grennell for the spring 1958 FAPA mailing, I recounted the early history of *Wild West Weekly* in some detail. Briefly, *WWW* was founded in 1902 (a date enshrined on the masthead in later years) as a five-cent weekly, a stable mate of such boys' magazines as *Pluck and Luck, Work and Win*, and *Fame and Fortune Weekly* published under the imprint of Frank Tousey, 168 West 23rd Street, New York, NY. Later the imprint became that of Harry E. Wolff, either an affiliate or a successor. On those early days, the magazine was a thin pamphlet whose closely printed pages were devoted largely to the novel-length adventures of a pulp hero named Young Wild West. No fewer than 52 novels featuring this redoubtable character appeared every year for perhaps two decades. They were of course, written by various hands, under the byline "An Old

Scout!" Although every one of these 1000 or more novels is probably virtually unreadable, I managed to read a couple of them and reported on Young Wild West in the *Grue* opus eluded to a moment ago.

In that same article, I also reported that Street and Smith bought me *Wild West Weekly* from the former publisher "in the early 1920's." However, further investigation seems to indicate that Street and Smith did not become the publisher until 1927. Indeed, Quentin Reynolds' history of Street and Smith, *The Fiction Factory* (Random House, 1955), says the event took place as late as 1929, though the appendix, giving publishing data on all Street and Smith titles, says 1927, and elsewhere Reynolds says *WWW* "was a success for 16 years," which would validate the authenticity of 1927 as the takeover date. At any event, during the early 1920's the magazine continued as a slim "Weekly," still featuring Young Wild West, but now only reprints of the old Tousey novels, printed from the old plates.

Street and Smith revamped the magazine in 1917, whether or not they had just taken over at that time. The old relic of the days of *Buffalo Bill* now appeared in regular pulp formal, the first issue dated August 13, 1927 or thereabouts. It sold for .10 and probably ran 112 shag-edged pages. It was edited by Ronald Oliphant, a Street and Smith veteran who had been connected with *Thrill Book* during its brief existence some years previously.

In the "new" *Wild West Weekly*, Young Wild West metamorphosed into Billy West, young part owner of the Circle J in Montana's Bitterroot Mountains. His saddle-mates, Cheyenne Charlie and Jim Dart, became Buck Foster and Joe Scott, and the two Chinese servants were lumped together into Sing Lo, Circle J's cook and handyman. Wild's "charming sweetheart," Arietta Murdock, became Ruth Dawe, part owner of Circle J, but she soon disappeared from the series, since the magazine aimed at younger readers, allowed very little "love interest" in its pages.

The original plan seems to have been to base the appeal of the magazine largely upon the exploits of Billy West, as the old Tousey magazine had been based largely on Young Wild West. For several years, the "Billy West" Novelette led off each issue. Later, the "Circle J" Novelette, as they were later called, appeared in perhaps eight of the ten issues, even though they seldom led the lineup. From around 1935 on, Circle J appeared in the magazine much less frequently.

Despite the desire to build the magazine on the popularity of Billy

West/Circle J, the editor of *Wild West Weekly* was careful to provide Circle J with a strong supporting case of "regular characters" who returned frequently, if not as frequently as Circle J. The earliest JW heroes were created by the editor himself, though the authors assigned to them worked out the details and plots themselves. Perhaps the earliest of these regulars was Bud Jones of Texas, a Ranger put through his paces by J. Allan Dunn, a well-known pulp writer who, like Ned Buntline, had led a colorful and adventurous life, and who looked, incidentally, like the old movie actor, Sir Guy Standing. Bud Jones of Texas appeared in the very first issue of the "new" *WWW*. Dunn also wrote about another regular character who began to appear with the first few issues, Pete Prentiss, the Whistlin' Kid, a Cattleman's Association range detective; these stories appeared under the penname of Emery Jackson, Kenneth Gilbert, later a slick writer of note, wrote about Ted Marsh of the Mounted, and one Reginald C. Barker wrote about Jim Hazel – Forest Ranger, under the pseudonym of Lee Harrington.

Other early regular characters included Lucius Carey, the Shootin' Fool, by Houston Irvine; Lum Yates, by Collins Hafford, Vincente the Yaqui, the Wilson Campbell; and Crosby Sheppard, the Ranny Kid, by Clee Woods. Most of these characters faded out of the picture by the mid-1930's, being replaced by newer and characters that were more popular although both Bud Jones and the Whistlin' Kid survived until about 1940, when J. Allan Dunn died.

According to Ronald Oliphant, who was the editor of the magazine from 1927 to 1939, "The magazine in its new form attracted favorable reader interest, and after perhaps three years the magazine was increased in size and the price upped to .15. The general appears of the magazine was improved, the crude covers of the .10 edition were replaced by better artwork, and the magazine built up a fairly good circulation for itself – considering that the country was getting well into the depression of the 1930's."

The magazine kept the .15 tag from about 1929 until August 10, 1935, when the price was reduced to .10. At the beginning, the magazine actually enlarged to 144 pages. The .10 edition of 1935 gave the reader 128 pages (or 130, counting the front cover, as was done later) until 1940, when the page count was cut to 114.

Undoubtedly among the chief factors in the popularity of the "new" *WWW* was the introduction of the new characters whose hard riding and straight shooting soon took the play away from the Circle J. Outfit. Kid Wolf and Sonny Tabor became by all odds the favorite characters of nearly all 3W readers, and they continued to appear with scarcely diminished popularity until the very end. Their original adventures (or an adaptation thereof) appeared in book form under the titles *Kid Wolf of Texas* and *Wanted: Sonny Tabor* in Chelsea House series published by Street and Smith; and Kid Wolf, at least, was the hero of a Big Little Book published in the 1930's. Both the Kid and Sonny were presented on radio for a brief while.

Sonny Tabor was apparently a later invention than Kid Wolf, who was already winning a huge following as early as mid-1929. Sonny did not arrive until a year or two later. He soon outstripped his older brain-brother in popularity, however, and by 1933, he was already undisputed king of the 3W range. Both characters were created by the same author, Paul S. Powers, under the penname of Ward M. Stevens. He also used this penname for a third series, featuring Freckles Malone, a pony express rider; but Freckles seldom appeared, although he was popular enough when he did show up. Possibly, it was difficult to work out fresh plots on the stereotyped pony express theme. At any rate, Freckles Malone was Powers' only qualified success.

As Andrew A. Griffin, Powers also created the cheerful and resourceful Johnny Forty-Five, another regular character who always rated among the top ten with 3W readers, and under his own byline during the final year of *WWW*'s existence, he created the Fightin' Three of the Rockin' T, who rated high although they had insufficient time to gather momentum before the magazine folded. As Griffin and under his own name, Powers also contributed numerous "independent" stories to *WWW*—stories not connected with a regular character—such as "The Legion of Wanted Men" and "Runt Madigan, Gun Lawyer." Powers was the Jack Williamson of *Wild West Weekly*. A prolific hack writer in the early days, he was able to grow with the magazine and hold his own among the somewhat more skillful scriveners who began to appear in the magazine in the 1940's. For the Christmas issue of 1941 Powers wrote a Sonny Tabor yarn, "Six-gun Santa," and added a touching little short, "Vigilante Christmas," that would make an excellent TV play for *Maverick*. Fittingly enough, the very last issue of the magazine (November 1943) contained two Powers novelettes.

Sonny Tabor's popularity proves again the potency of the Billy the Kid legend for Tabor was unabashedly a replica modeled on the New Mexican outlaw as popularly conceived. Unjustly accused of a murder, Sonny is faced to a life on the dodge, with a $6,000 reward posted for his capture or demise. Of course, he is actually a model of deportment and spends most of his time running down the actual criminals who committed the crimes of which he is accused. Like Billy the Kid, Sonny would not be driven from his home range, in his case Arizona rather than New Mexico, and probably unlike the Kid, he wore the same clothes at all times, which made it easy for people to recognize him, possibly even at night when the wind was right. Sonny's extreme youth and innocence was accentuated by "a bullet scar on one bronzed cheek that had more than once been taken for a babyish dimple." Aside from this, and the conventional attributes of the fastest gun and the straightest aim in the West, Sony hardly required gimmicks and eccentricities to make him famous.

In contract, Kid Wolf ("Kid to mah friends, Wolf to mah enemies") was a more conventional pulp hero, artfully gimmicked up and fitted with a set of eccentricities to make him colorful and distinctive. Although he professed great longing for the "Rio" country of Texas, he was independently wealthy and spent his life seeking adventure in all parts of the west from the "snow country" to old Mexico. He proclaimed himself "a friend of the undah dag" and was wont to remark, "Yo' see, down in Texas where I come from they call me the 'soldiah of Misfohtune.' I'm proud of that name, and only wished I deserved it mo'." As you will note, he always spoke in sort of an ersatz southern dialect. His garb was colorful if not usually utilitarian; he wore fringed buckskin like Kit Carson or Daniel Boone, a huge sombrero with the front of it pinned back to the crown, and two Cold Peacemakers .45's. In addition to these weapons, he toted a "hideout", a Bowie knife sheathed inside his shirt between his shoulder blades, which he could reach back and grab his knife and hurl it with blinding speed before a gunman with a cold drop could squeeze a trigger.

Johnny Forty-Five wasn't merely eccentric; he was plain *meshuggah*. He habitually rolled a cigarette with his right hand, then another with his left, and then threw both away unsmoked. (He must have been followed by bums wherever he went, though his last was not specified). His explanation for this practice is also characteristic of him. To his partner George Krumm he would say something like this:

"It keeps my fingers nimble, George,
And I'm surely not a-jokin';
My hands they roll the quirlies,

And my guns, they do the smokin'."

Johnny probably owed most of his popularity to Krumm. "Fearless" George Krumm, self-styled Terror of Evildoers, tipped the beam at 200+ pounds (fat, not muscle) and "always rode with all the fire, grace, and abandon of a bag of sand." On one memorable occasion, he chugalugged a bottle of Tabasco sauce under the impression it was a bottle or rare wine. On another occasion, receiving a letter from his superior containing secret orders and ending, "After memorizing the contents of this letter, be sure and incinerate it immediately," George mused, "The chief don't seem to realize how dangerous it would be if this here letter was found on me. I'm takin' my life in my hands, carryin' it around this way. I've got a good notion to *burn* it."

Powers fathered all these raffish characters and kept them going full-tilt for a decade and more, but other writers were more prolific. One of the leading 3W hacks was Lee Bond, though he seems to have died or given up his art sometime in the early 1940s. As Cleve Endicott, he wrote most of the Circle J novelettes; as has been pointed out, Circle J appeared nearly every week for six or eight years, so this was a sizeable stint in itself. As Lee Bond, he wrote countless "single" stories, nearly all of novelette length, such as "Feud Range" and "Bullet Brand," and contributed frequent stories about two regular characters. One of these was among the leading 3W heroes, Jack Reese, the Oklahoma Kid, no relation to nay other Oklahoma Kids elsewhere, an outlaw who defied 3W tradition by being as homely as sin rather than bronzed and handsome, and who was perpetually pursued by a popeyed deputy sheriff named Ed Sparks, perpetually armed with a mighty, double-barreled shotgun. Bond also wrote a series of short stories about Calamity Boggs, a chronic pessimist and hypochondriac, no relation.

It should be pointed out that there existed a hierarchy of regular characters in *WWW*, with position based largely on popularity and signified by such things as frequency of appearance, place in the magazine and above all by the length of the story. The titans, Kid Wolf, Sonny Tabor, Johnny Forty-Five, the Oklahoma Kid, and various others were never allowed to appear except in novelette-length stories, which were nearly always featured on the front cover. Lesser characters such as Calamity Boggs, Lum Yates, the Shootin' Fool, Shorty Masters, Jim Hazel, and others, appeared only in short stories. Between these extremes were a few characters that sometimes appeared in novelettes but most often in short stories, Hungry and Rusty, Bud Jones, the Whistlin' Kid, and Jimmy Quick were some of them. Of course, social mobility existed even in 3W and some characters rose and fell as time went on. Shorty Masters, M.D. (Mule Driver), made his final 3W appearance in novelette form in the early 1940's, after appearing only in short stories for a decade, though possibly his rise was partly as a result of the growing prestige of his author, Allan R. Bosworth, (See Bosworth's amusing article "The Golden Age of Pulps" in *The Atlantic*, July, 1961. He mentions his authorship of 200 Shorty Masters stories during the 1930s).

William F. Bragg, perhaps one of the most talented of *WWW* contributors, created two popular characters, Silver Jack Steele and Flash Moran, who got along without any gimmicks or eccentricities, although the former did flaunt a white lock of hair where once a charge of buckshot had nicked his scalp. Bragg later created a series of stories about a character named Highpockets Halligan, which was part of a sudden emphasis on humor in *WWW* during the late 1930s. Allan R. Bosworth under pennames wrote several humorous series, including one about Judge Roy Bean and another about a pair named Jeff and Bugeye. Another such series was Hinges Hollister, by Phil Squires. However, all these intentionally humorous series were a bit tiresome, and Bragg himself did much better with humorous touches in stories not presented as humor. He wrote a number of stories about a character named Andy Irons, including two that rank among the finest stories ever published in *Wild West Weekly*, "Trouble from Texas" and "Ridin' the Roarin' Chinook." The latter was tastefully spiced with a dash of wild humor involving Captain Andrew Jackson Irons, young Andy's hell-for-leather father.

Andy Irons, despite occasional appearances over at least eight or ten years, never made the pantheon as a bonafide regular character. There were others like him, including George C. Henderson's Bullwhip Adams, Hal Davenport's Banty Red Watkins, and William A. Todd's Risky McKee. A real 3W regular was indicated in at least one, and usually all, of three ways, (1) His next adventure was forecast in the "Comin' Next Week!" house ad in a notice like this one for "Murder Trail" by J. Allan Dunn, "Bud Jones of Texas rides again an shows by his special brand o' gun play thet he ain't fergot none o' the tricks of his dangerous trade, Rangerin'." (2) At the end of his current adventure, there was an editorial note, promising another story about the character very soon now, "When a gent kin handle outlaws like thet, yuh kin' bet your bottom dollar he's due back in Street and Smith's *Wild West Weekly* pronto…Don't miss the next Silver Jack Steele adventure." (3) And most importantly of all, the regular character always visited "The Wranglers Corner" each time he appeared in the magazine.

"The Wranglers Corner" began in the first issue of the "new" *WWW* and continued every week for a decade and more. It was the letter department of the magazine until about 1937, when it became an amateur writers' department. Throughout these years, it functioned as a sort of *Wild West* version of a Justice League of America meeting where the 3W regulars congregated, talked shop, and listened to the letters from "the readin' hombres." Evidently written by the editor, "The Wranglers Corner" usually boasted a little narrative to flavor it, sometimes a slight plot, and its characters were all the bonafide regulars whose adventures appeared in that particular issue of the magazine.

Once a character was invited to "The Wranglers Corner", he was indisputably in the pantheon although in later years the rules were occasionally relaxed to admit some riffraff. Various characters such as Frank J. Litchfield's Jimmy Quick appeared now and then for years before achieving membership in the "Corner." A few regulars "made" it on their very first appearance; however, these characters usually came to *WWW* from other places, Pete Rice, by Austin Gridley, became a 3W regular soon after his own magazine, *Pete Rice Western*, folded up. Hal Dunning's Jim Twin Allen, the White Wolf, had appeared in several Chelsea House books (and presumably in another Street and Smith magazine) before he arrived in *WWW*. All his 3W appearances were authored by Walker Tompkins under the Dunning byline, the creator of the character having died some years previously.

Walker Tompkins was one of *Wild West Weekly's* most prolific and popular writers from the early 1930's to mid-1942 when he was inducted into the service during World War II. He wrote under various pennames and house names, most notably Philip F. Deere, but under his own handle, he created the perennial favorite, Tommy Rockford, he of the golden handcuffs, who was first a railroad detective, later a border patrolman. (In the former capacity he seldom went near a railroad; as soon as he switched to the latter trade he immediately became involved in a railroad robbery). The early Rockford novelettes such as "The Navajo Avenger" and "Skulls in Wrist Canyon," were of particular merit and interest because they were primarily detective stories in a western setting. Later Rockford degenerated into a conventional shoot-'em-up lawman.

Despite Tommy Rockford's fame, Walker Tompkin's niche in the 3W Hall of Fame was won, not by his authorship of the Rockford stories but by his status as the leading creator of six-story series. "All Stories Complete" was the cover slogan and editorial policy of *Wild West Weekly* for many years. Possibly, it was inaugurated because young readers, who constituted the bulk of the 3W readership, are deemed less likely than that of an adult, to read "long" stories of serial length. However, serials are traditionally a publisher's method of strengthening a reader's loyalty to his magazine, and presumably, the front office declared in favor of "continued" stories. At any rate, a happy compromise was achieved when in the early 1930's Editor Oliphant developed what was called the six-story series, a set of six novelettes, each complete in itself but with a close tie-in with the preceding yarns. Such series featured the same hero or heroes, the same villain or villains, and the same general setting and circumstances. Thus, taken together, the set of six stories comprised a serial of six installments each complete in itself.

Unlike most *WWW* stories, these six-story series often boasted, "love interest," and often featured golden-haired heroes who could be kidnapped and rescued once in each story. Each of the six stories ended with the hero victorious in one phase of his struggle against the villains in much the same way that Kim Kinnison triumphed at the end of the "Lensman" novel. Usually the story climaxed with the death of a secondary villain or in the supposed death of the top villain, whose real identity might be a mystery. Only a very stupid reader, of course, could believe that the top villain was actually dead for keeps when he beheld the editorial note at the end of the story promising further adventures of the hero in an upcoming issue, but at least the story was technically complete in itself.

The original six-story series formula was followed with apparent success down to around 1936 or 1937, after which decadence set in and the six-story series became merely a set of six stories about a particular hero who was pitted against six different villains in different settings and circumstances. Various heroes of six-story series won enough reader interest and support to return in two or more series, and sometimes came back, at last, as regular characters. Senor Red Mask, created by Guy L. Maynard, was on of these. He first appeared in a six-story series about 1932, came back for two or three encores, and finally became a permanent fixture. He owed most of his popularity to his colorful trappings, the garb of a wealthy Mexican caballero—and the equally colorful border atmosphere of the tales.

Another regular who was originally introduced in a six-story series was Trig Trenton, the Border Eagle, first introduced in 1933 and the hero of two further six-story series in 1935 and 1937 before becoming a regular. These stories were written by Walker Tompkins under the house name of Philip F. Deere, but while the Border Eagle was perhaps Tompkins' most successful character after Tommy Rockford in terms of longevity, these stories were by no means his major contribution to the six-story canon. Probably two such series qualify for that honor, "Terror Trail" and "The Desert Phantom," both written by Tompkins under his own name. The Phantom, alluded to above, first appeared in a six-story cycle in 1933, and was brought back for an encore in 1935. The original was an excellent and colorful saga of masked vengeance, but the sequel was very dull and ordinary, most of the magic having dissipated when the hero's face was unmasked.

The "Terror Trail" series was later rewritten as a novel and published in book form, but no sequel was possible because the setting, rather than its plot or characters, was its chief attraction. Most of the action took place in an authentic Spanish castle hidden in "a remote fastness of the Rocky Mountains." It had been built by Don Picadero, "a notorious buccaneer of the conquistador period...to be his hideout and the storing place of all his ill-gotten gains." The series ended with part of the treasure recovered and the Rio Torcido flooding the bottled-up canyon wherein the castle stood, forming "a lost lake pooled between windswept pines" and hiding the "grim secret" beneath its placid surface. "Only the wild ducks and moaning pines know about it, and they will never tell." The book version of "Terror Trail" did not include this passage, and I was mightily disappointed. Tompkins wrote many other excellent six-story series, including "Cougar Fang," "Deputy Death," and "The Arizona Thunderbolt," but none was as off trail as these.

William F. Bragg was hardly less successful in selling six-story series than Tompkins himself. He wrote two or three series about Starr of Wyoming, the first especially fine, and many others about other characters. One was called Trail Blazer, another Maverick—no connection with the TV series of many years later, to mention a few at random, Guy L. Maynard (with "Far-away Logan"), William A. Todd (with "Ronny Fellows"), Andrew A. Griffin (with "Senor Mystery"), and George C. Henderson (with "Whizz Fargo") were other six-story authors of note. There were many others.

During the golden years, the usual formula for an issue of *WWW* was a table of contents composed of three novelettes and four (or occasionally five) short stories. Usually all the novelettes were devoted to the adventures of regular characters or six-story series characters, and two or three of the shorts also concerned regulars. This meant that in a given issue there were five to seven regulars on hand. The idea used later by the Justice League of America in which various heroes banded together within the bounds of a single story, was used with caution in *Wild West Weekly*, though there were always reader demands for more "combination" stories. Apparently, the earliest experiment along this line took place shortly before I bought my first issue, it featured Circle J and Sonny Tabor in a single rip-roaring novelette. The same characters met again the following year in the issue for April 7, 1934, the story being titled "Sonny Tabor Fights for Circle J." Circle J was a favorite for such combinations because it was written under a house name, and a single author could "collaborate" with himself to produce a story. The stories in which Circle J met Sonny Tabor and later Kid Wolf were bylined Cleve Endicott and Ward M. Stevens, but were written entirely by Paul S. Powers. Circle J also adventured with the Whistlin' Kid, the Bar U Twins, and probably others. Various other regulars joined forces on occasion, but probably the most famous occasion of all was in the September 7, 1935 issue, which featured Ward M. Stevens' "Kid Wolf Rounds up Sonny Tabor." Despite the dominance of regular characters there were sometimes "independent" novelettes and quite often short stories not devoted to any regular characters. Walker Tompkins, Lee Bond, and other prolific writers pounded them out between other assignments. Mention should be made of the immensely popular novelettes that appeared under the bylines of William A. Todd and of Ben Conlon. Todd's most famous yarns included "The Secret of Sundown Mesa," "The Shooting of Trigger Kane," and "The Gun Curse of Solo Dale," while Ben Conlon, who never wrote about "regular," penned such outstanding "stray" novelettes as "Smoky Clark – Trial Boss," already mentioned above, "The Gun Boss," and "A Deputy for Salamander." Whether Todd and Conlon were genuine or only pennames or house names for other writers, I do not know. I remember looking for their stories with the same interest that, in later years, I glanced over the contents page of *Astounding* for the stories of A.E. van Vogt and Anson MacDonald (Robert A. Heinlein).

The Last Years, 1939-1943

Inevitably, according to the inexorable laws of economics, *Wild West Weekly* changed a little when the price was cut from .15 to .10 a copy with the issue of August 10, 1935. Sixteen shag-edged pages were topped off; one of the three regular departments, "Western Pen Pals" conducted by Sam Wills, was dropped, and the two remaining departments, "Fiddlin' Joe's Song Corral" and "The Wranglers Corner," were reduced in size and set in smaller type. However, the biggest change lay in the fact that one of the usual "Four Complete Western Stories" in each issue was now done in comic-strip form. These stories ran in "complete episodes" but like six-story series, taken together told a more or less continued story. They ran for about 20 installments before being dropped for a fresh "story in pictures," though some characters returned for an encore. For about four years, these comic-strip yarns consisted of pictures with a brief text underneath, as the popular "Tarzan" feature in the daily newspapers, but during the final year of the feature the text was dropped and the story was told with hand letter captions and balloons in the panels themselves. When the latter format was adopted, a byline was added at last, Warren E. Carleton, previously no byline had been visible. However, William Timmins, later cover artist for *Astounding*, drew the strips throughout the entire five years, and quite completely, too, using several styles and techniques.

The first comic-strip character in *WWW* was Dogie Cantwell; the last, Omaha Hooker. In between came Brazos Bell, Fargo Neal, Slim Harkness, Sailor Anson, Dusty Radburn, and several other forgettable characters. The "story in pictures" feature was dropped forever early in 1940.

The changes that took place in 1935 were minor compared with those that came a few years later. By the late 1930's, the magazine was beginning to feel the pinch. Radio, movies, and particularly the burgeoning comic books were beginning to kill off the pulps. Street and Smith tried to meet the challenge by improving the physical appeal of the magazine. A new logo was designed and run superimposed on the cover painting, as was never done in earlier times. A year or two later the contents page layout was revamped. The result looked more modern and streamlined, but it resulted in the disappearance of the familiar years. I never quite forgave them for that. Trimmed edges showed up about the end of 1939, only to halfway disappear again with the final issues of 1943, which boasted only the sides trimmed, top and bottom still shaggy.

Following the time-honored custom, a new editor was brought to retool the magazine in 1939. He was John Burr, who also edited *Western Story* and probably other Street and Smith pulps. Though his regime proved to be in a minor way comparable with that of Sam Merwin, Jr., at *TWS* and *Startling* late in the 1940's, most 3W fans and probably many 3W authors lamented the departure of Ronald Oliphant, always deemed a fair and friendly editor.

Under Burr, *WWW* was allowed to "mature" somewhat, though it was still aimed at younger readers and not intended to compete with *Western Story*. The most welcome innovation of the new regime was the use of more nearly correct English in the magazine. In former times, blurbs, editorial notes, departments, and even many story titles were rendered in a semi-literate western lingo calculated to drive and halfway intelligent reader away screaming in short order. This lingo was drastically toned down beginning in 1939, though it never quite disappeared entirely.

His Wranglers Corner" had been turned into an amateur writer's department about 1937, but continued to serve as the meeting place of 3W regular characters till 1939 when that gimmick was dropped. The department itself continued into 1940 but thereafter, it was dropped for good. "Fiddlin' Joe's Song Corral", an early manifestation of an interest in folk music, a department dating back to the beginning of the Street and Smith *WWW*, had been dropped shortly before. Editor Oliphant had instituted a brief editorial department called "A Chat with the Range Boss" late in 1938; this published comments on current and upcoming stories, as well as letters from authors and readers, and for a time was the only department in the magazine. In mid-1941, however, a new letter column, "Readers' Branding Irons," was instituted, and lasted as long as the magazine.

Better artwork had begun to appear in the late 1930's when H.W. Scott began to be squeezed out by Bjorklund, a superior western illustrator who did most of the interiors from about 1937 to 1940. In the same era, *WWW* adopted the full-page "book jacket" illustrations, which became a standard feature in all Street and Smith pulps including *Astounding and Unknown*, for a year or two. By 1940, *WWW* was an extremely attractive pulp, boasting trimmed edges, superior illustrations, and modern logo and titles. It remained an attractive pulp to the end, but in mid-1941, old-time readers could see that the magazine was falling on lean times. All the artwork in the magazine, cover and interiors, was now reprint material. The covers were all taken form the *WWW* files for the 1930's. The interiors presumably were selected from the files of *Western Story, Cowboy Stories,* and other Street and Smith Western magazines of the past, since *WWW* itself had too many Scott illustrations and too few worthy drawings in its back files. Western fiction is stereotyped enough so that drawings in the files could be found to illustrate almost any story after a fashion. The final *WWW* issues in 1943 seem to have been specifically illustrated again, all drawings done by an artist named Smith.

Under John Burr, drastic experiments were undertaken in the fiction department. IN 1939, serials were allowed for the first time, beginning with William F. Bragg's "Tiedown Johnny's Gunsmoke Trail," which read as though it had originally been conceived or written as a six-story series and converted to serial form. However, several notable serials were printed, including Alan R. Bosworth's "Steel to the Sunset" and Walker Tompkins' "Trail of the Iron Horse," serials managed only indifferent success, and the ancient "All Stories Complete" policy was reaffirmed about 1941.

"Independent" novelettes and short stories were allowed far more space than they had been given in the 1930's, and during 1939-1941, the cast of regulars was almost crowded out by serials and "stray" stories. Various new characters were introduced to replace old favorites who were losing popularity, and some of these remained to compete with the old regulars during the final years of the magazine. Perhaps the most important of these new regulars were Rowdy Lang and Black Solone, outlaw and man-hunter respectively, who corresponded roughly with Sonny Tabor and Kid Wolf, and like those characters were the creations of a single writer, one James P. Webb.

The other newcomers who managed to achieve major status in *WWW* were relatively few in number, Clay Starr introduced Dapper Donnelly, patent medicine salesman, Ed Earl Repp created Yuma Bill Storms and his partner, Beanpole Badger; J.F. Houghton wrote a series of "humorous" shorts about Cameron Glaflin and Chuck Martin chronicled the adventures of Rawhide Runyan ("his neighbors called him a cowboys' cowboy!"). As was mentioned many pages ago, Paul S. Powers added to his string of regulars in 1942 by introducing the Fightin' Three of the Rockin' T.

The requests in "Readers' Branding Irons" clamored for the old favorites, and the "Range Boss" was forced to explain on several occasions "we're bringing back the old favorites as often as we can." He pointed out that "some authors just aren't available." Apparently, he referred to writers who had died and that others had retired. Some writers such as Allan R. Bosworth had gone up to the slicks. Sonny Tabor, Kid Wolf, Johnny Forty-Five, Circle J., Hungry and Rusty, the White Wolf, Tommy Rockford, the Border Eagle, Senor Red Mask, the Oklahoma Kid, Silver Jack Steele, and Flash Moran were the chief characters from the old days who survived to the last.

These old favorites were somewhat "de-corned" for the new era in which they ventured. Kid Wolf's "southern drawl" was toned down, and Sonny Tabor may even have changed his checkered shirt for the first time in history. Sonny spent several years acting as an undercover lawman, having won a pardon, a girlfriend, and a saddle buddy, about 1939, but during the last year of the magazine, 1943, he became a bonafide man-on-the-dodge again. As far as I know, however, even under the "mature" influence of the new regime nobody was ever told the Christian names of "Kid" Wolf and "Sonny" Tabor, or for that matter, of "Buck" Foster, "Hungry" Hawkins, "Rusty" Bolivar, "Trig" Trenton, or "Flash" Moran. I suspect that even their creators did not have this information available.

The evil day was put off longer than anyone should have confidently expected, but in the summer of 1943, *WWW* failed to appear on its weekly schedule for probably the first time in its 41-year history. The last word in its title was whacked off, and the magazine became a monthly publication, known as *Wild West*. About five monthly issues, priced at .15 and enlarged to 146 pages, later to only 130, appeared before the final blow fell without warning on page 29 of the November 1943 issue, "Because of the drastic necessity for the conservation of paper and because we are doing everything in our power to cooperate without government in winning this war, we announce, with regrets, that with this issue *Wild West* will suspend publication for the duration..." This notice appeared in the middle of "Death Blots the Brands," a Fightin' Three novelette by Paul S. Powers. The only other regulars who made the final issue were the Oklahoma Kid and Johnny Forty-Five. If *Wild West* hadn't died as a war casualty, of course, TV would have killed it along with the rest of the pulps within another five or six years, but perhaps it is fitting that *WWW* (or *WW*) died, as it were, with its boots on. Some of the first stories to appear included Billy West in "West of Circle J"; Kid Wolf No. 1 was published November 3, 1928, Sonny Tabor No. 1 on July 6, 1929, and Johnny Forty-Five, May 24, 1930. The first combined story was "Circle J Trails Sonny Tabor" on March 18, 1933. The second one was "Sonny Tabor

Fights for Circle J." A third tale appeared in 1940, by J. Allen Dunn & Emery Jackson, who were the same man. He also wrote under the name John B. Strong. The inside drawings were done by H.W. Scott until May 9, 1936 when a new artist started. His name was Larry Bjorklund, and his first was "Outlaw's Dollar" with Risky McGee.

The Bar U–Circle J story was written by Charles Barnes, and Kid Wolf and Sonny Tabor by Paul S. Powers under the penname of Ward M. Stevens, on February 23, 1935. The Whistlin' Kid's "Circle J Pards" appeared on August 15, 1936; Pete Rice rides down Sonny Tabor February 4, 1939. The third Kid Wolf & Sonny Tabor Saddle Mates, "Kid Wolf Law on Circle J," was in 1940; a Pete Rice & Sonny Tabor Story was published in 1939. Lee Bond wrote the first Oklahoma Kid story (March 7, 1933), called "Thet Ugly Little Hombre."

To end this article I must briefly mention the 3W Club that grew up during the last years among the ardent letterbacks in "Readers' Branding Irons." Among the most fannish of these fans are David C. Sparks, Bill James, Marion Henderson, Jack Powers (the son, I believe, of Paul S.), Bill Foster, and others. But the Number One 3W Fan by general acclaim was Bob Stratton of Seattle, Washington, who owned a vast collection, many if not all of the 2,118 issues published over 41 years and was a walking encyclopedia of 3W lore. Bob had entered the armed services during World War II but he was killed in action. Thus, ironically, *Wild West Weekly* and its most passionate admirer died almost at the same time.

Note:

As I did at the end of the *Grue* article about Young Wild West and Circle J, I must acknowledge the help I received in writing this article from Walker Tompkins, one of *WWW*'s most famous contributors, and Ronald Oliphant, *WWW* editor from 1927 to 1939. Many thanks to both of them.

– Redd Boggs.

A final note before we leave *Wild West Weekly*. "Fiddlin' Joe's Song Corral" is proving to be a rich source of serious folk song material. This information was provided me by ex-pulpster Ben Haas, now living and writing Westerns in Austra.

The person responsible for "Fiddlin' Joe's Corner" was Thea Wheelwright:

"I was then a high school graduate barely nineteen years old and hired by Blackwell as an experiment to see whether I could function along with the Vassar graduates who were acting as editors in various magazines there. We used to all gather for lunch at Charles' down on 6ᵗʰ Avenue, a luncheon which usually went on for much longer than an hour, until the efficiency experts who were hired to help Street and Smith compete with rising competition from such publishers as Dell, put up time clocks, much to our chagrin."

Today, Ms. Wheelwright has her own publishing firm in Freeport, Maine.

"My home run was *Ranch Romances*"

— Harold Hersey, *Pulpwood Editor*

The Romance Western

"Leather, sweat, raw whiskey, and gunfire, put some girls in if you want, but people don't go to a Western movie to see the girls."

— Elmore Leonard, personal correspondence

Two types of Western pulp magazines equaled Street and Smith's two big hits, *Wild West Weekly* and *Western Story Magazine*. The super hero Western pulp magazines such as *The Rio Kid* have found a new life after death, and are the most sought after Western pulp magazine collectibles today, and the love-type pulps such as *Ranch Romances* would equal the sales of the Street and Smith magazines and outlive them in the marketplace.

In spite of the learned opinion of many excellent Western writers, I must confess a disdain for much of the soft-core sex with side orders of movie talk, trailside cookbook stuff, and pen pal mishmash that the love or romance Western turned out.

Marshall McLuhan talks about the dichotomy between the horse opera and the soap opera (The Mechanical Bride). In the horse opera, there is complete masculine freedom and a total absence of the personal and domestic problems that form the nucleus of the soap opera. The love Western pulp was more soap opera than horse opera.

The heroes of the love Western pulps were more sob sisters than gutsy daughters of the dime novel in the tradition of Hurricane Nell, Calamity Jane, and Montana Kate who had been significant improvement over the passive leather-stocking females. While one might be tempted on the

strength of this to speculate that this type of fiction would not sell to today's more liberated female reader, it's clear that the romance is alive and well and flourishing in Toronto (Harlequin Romances), and in many other places (Dell's Candlelight love novels, Silhouette Romances, the Second Chance at Love series, etc.).

The April 19, 1974 *Wall Street Journal* chronicled the story of Harlequin Enterprises, Ltd., a Canadian publishing house that features pulp-type romantic fiction where "the virtuous heroine has been swept off her feet by a dashing suitor." All this is accomplished with *no* violence and

only a hint of sex. The chaste kiss and the promise to live happily married ever after are the lifeblood of the Harlequin books. The Romance Western pulps were similarly oriented, with relatively sexless, over-sentimentalized, soap-operish stories in Western settings.

The Harlequin covers are described by the Journal reporter thusly, "Each book is like the last...printed on cheap paper with a brightly colored cover showing the fair maid demurely glancing at her ruggedly handsome hero," and so forth. If all of this is not proof enough of the durability of the pulp theme, recently a paperback was published bearing the title *Western Romances*, a collection of pulp and slick Western romance stories, reprinted mainly from the 1940's and 1950's. This was a one-shot publication. The pulp covers likewise featured fair maidens in dire peril – of achieving matrimony, their only apparent interest.

I confess to a bias in Western yarns for the bone-cracking, slap-leather style, with a strong hero, a badass villain, and female presences representative of real frontier towns. However, in actual fact the sweet little lasses of *Ranch Romances* (subtitled *Love Stories of the Real West*) long outlived all the "Kids" at the corner newsstand, an example, no doubt of fiction imitating life, with the certain victory of marriage its resulting domestication of the lonesome cowpoke.

"For he was startling, even in appearance. His clothes presented a perfect symphony in black. From sombrero to boots, including the mask, his apparel was absolutely uncompromising in its blackness. His stallion itself shared the color – a mount as glossily black as a Nedjae colt. To complete the bizarre effect, he wore a long Mexican cloak, which flowed over him in voluminous black folds. It concealed the lines of his figure; and when he rode fast, it usually billowed out behind him fantastically, like the wings of a monstrous bat."
— *The Masked Rider*

The Hero Western

"In a land where the only law was the law of the gun, the masked rider made his own laws, and meted out justice with strong, fair hands." Death's Head Vengeance."
— *The Lone Ranger Magazine*

While the trappers, cattlemen, and ranchers were the significant Western frontier influences, and a certain settling-in effect was provided by the family and its institutions, the schools and churches, the real excitement of the frontier was embodied in its heroes, both real and fictional. On the real frontier, it was Hardin, Earp, and the James brothers in the pulp Westerns it was The Lone Ranger, El Halcon, and The Rio Kid.

Editors soon discovered that strong, hero-type Western characters had a greater reader interest potential than garden-variety ones; the former tended to gain a certain amount of "brand loyalty." As one editor of the period puts it, "The advantages were evident; instead of fragmenting his creativity on a variety of heroes, the writer could concentrate on building and enlarging on and every reader who was captured by that one would be sent back in search of the earlier stories he had missed as well as being a pre-sold customer for the next, far more than if he merely happened to like the author." It was a simple formula but a proven one. Therefore, the word was out to the writers, especially to the Thrilling, Double-Action, and Street and Smith stables.

The pulp Western super hero, although not possessed of superhuman or supernatural powers, was a cut above the ordinary mortal. He could absorb more than his share of punishment, more in the fashion of his cousins in the hard-boiled detective genre. He was characterized by immediate action in response to a dilemma or conflict, which was always external, a burned-out ranch, or a murdered friend. Some call this kind of writing morality plays, others "horse opera." Those who purchased the Western hero magazines mainly lusted after solid adventure/action yarns. The following is typical of the hero pulps, as taken from *Lead and Flame,* a "Walt Slade" novel by Bradford Scott, in the January 1947 issue of *Thrilling Western:*

> His nerves taut as stretched wire, Walt Slade stared downward. The splintered wreck of the bridge swayed drunkenly in the wind, rasping against the rock, the broken girders cracking and straining. They hung by the ragged shreds of tough wood that had beet instead of breaking.
>
> Slade's mind worked at racing speed. To attempt to clamber down the wreck would be plain lunacy; but unless something was done quickly, Brant would perish. The struggle attendant to returning to consciousness would certainly slide his body from the upright, even if the dangling fragment of the bridge did not fall first. Slade whirled about and whistled to Shadow. The black horse trotted to him, snorting, and trembling. Slade swiftly un-looped his rope and tied hard and fast to the saddle horn. "If the cinches bust, it'll be all up with Brant and me, but we got to risk it," the Hawk muttered. "It's up to you to stand fast, Shadow."
>
> Slade's hands were torn and bleeding, his muscles seemed turned to water. Sweat poured from him and he shook as with ague. The heavy weight upon his shoulder bore down with ever-increasing force. His breath came in chocking gasps. All the while bullets were whining overhead or spitting against the far wall of the gorge. Let one strike the straining horse and it would be all over in a minute.
>
> A rosy, bubbling mist formed before Slade's eyes. His ears roared to the pounding of his pulse. One hand slipped and he all but lost his hold on the rope. Then, dazedly, as if in a nightmare, he felt the ragged lip of stone against his

fingers. A convulsive tug and he was lying on firm ground, retching and gasping.

Needless to say, the Hawk, an undercover Texas Ranger, would survive and prevail in spite of all his difficulties.

The first appearance of El Halcon was in the Street and Smith *Wild West Weekly*, and he was at that time a bandit adversary of Senor Red Mask (Author, Guy Maynard):

> A burly form rushed at Senor Red Mask out of the murk of battle. "El Halcon! It's him or me, now!" cried the desperate caballero.

> Crash! Bang! Senor Red Mask's hot guns rocketed lead and flame. El Halcon—The Hawk of the Rio Grande staggered. He was hit. Still he lunged forward. He seemed to bear a charmed life. Snarling bitter oaths, he gripped his guns for a deadly blast at close range.

Volume 1, Number 1 of *The Western Raider* (August-September 1938) introduced the Rio Robin Hood, Alias Silver Trent, "You may hear the legend by lonely campfires along the dim trails, where hard men curse, in admiration or in fear, at this name." Silver Trent had the principal assets, fast hands, as well as a handsome physique, and an adversary named El Diablo, whom he would pursue over the short life of his magazine. The most interesting feature of this pulp was not Silver Trent, however, but an anti-hero pair. The Texas Dude and The Tomcat Kid, who were all the things they shouldn't have been ugly, drunken, unwilling to let the worthy opposition draw first in a showdown. The author, Tom Roan, even gave the Tomcat Kid a large set of buckteeth. These were not stock Western pulp characters, and were most unusual for the time:

> The Texas Dude and the Tomcat Kid had the advantage. Hell, it was no time for ethics, whatever that was! They had simply opened fire without taking the trouble to start making a lot of noise about it before their guns started off and the men were falling in front of them.

When *The Western Raider* folded, Silver continued to pursue El Diablo in the pages of *Star Western*.

The Rio Kid (featuring Bob Prior and His Fighting Pards) by C. William Harrison, Tom Curry and Don David, was a novel-length creation of the Thrilling group, appearing in *The Rio Kid Western*; this was a twist on the typical pulp Western yarn in that the fictional characters such as John Slaughter, and real locations such as the O.K. Corral.

The Kid's only weapons against the "hopeless odds of outlawry" were an ever-present smile (variously described as an icy stare, enigmatic grin, thin grin, faint hard smile), a pair of Colts which, when pressed into action, "leaped out like striking snakes," and a "wonder" horse. The Kid could polish them off with the best of them, with classic psychopathic indifference:

> "Dan yuh, Pryor! Take it then."
>
> His gun flashed from under his coat in a blue blur, but death had struck him before he could cock the hammer. His savage violence sustained a terrific jolt, as Pryor's slug plowed through his check. Blood came to the front of his shirt, widened rapidly, and he looked at it dazedly. All the stiffness drained swiftly from his body then. His head rolled, his eyes fading. He swayed off balance, took a long loose step, and then went down to the floor in a crumpled heap. The Rio Kid stood there motionlessly until the last echoes of his shot had faded into the darkness that shrouded Tombstone's broad streets, and then slowly he sheathed his gun, and lifted his eyes to Chip Malloy's gray face.
>
> "When I came here I saw Lucy waitin' at the hotel," he said quietly. "She'll be worried if yuh don't show up soon."

This particular story, *Gun Legion* (February 1942), was set in Tombstone; the shootout took place in the Crystal Palace, and the Kid was drawn as a latter-day Doc Holliday, tasked with "cleaning up the town. With the help of paperback reprints, *The Rio Kid* ran from October 1934 to the early 1970's.

Don Muerte (Gentleman of Death) was Star Western's (and Harry Olmstead's) contribution to the long list of Western superheroes. Don

Muerte, son of an Irish Adventurer who had been executed by powerful ranchers, was out to humble these arrogant overlords "until the lot of the common man was made a matter of smiles instead of tears." To accomplish his goal, Don Muerte "would teach the peons" ninos all the tricks of the knife, the pistol, and the saddle carbine." Ray Nafziger came up with another hero-type series centering about the Hooker Brothers of Canyon Lobo, a succession of stories tied together by common characters and locales.

The Pulp Western superhero operated just inside the law, and was fashioned after Edward L. Whee'er's Deadwood Dick, the Black Rider of the Black Hills, described by Daryl Jones as "a deadly shot and skilled equestrian, a master in the art of disguise. He cleverly evades pursuit or tracks down villains, tasks facilitated by a guaranteed income of five thousand dollars a year from his own gold mind. Forever young, handsome and chivalrous, Deadwood Dick brings a blush to the cheeks of the beautiful and yearning women who abound in the novels."

The Masked Rider (of *Masked Rider Western*) was a Thrilling super hero in the Deadwood Dick tradition that a long string of writers would work over the years, including Oscar Schisgall (it is his description at the beginning of this section), Oscar J. Friend, Hascal Giles, Lee Wells, Charles N. Heckelmann, and master of weird fiction, Joseph Payne Brennan. Often editors would have a variety of writers do a single story and would ask for reader opinion as to who should continue to work the series (Who said there was no pressure in writing for the Pulps?).

While the early Masked Rider stories were better pulp yarns, the dialogue had regressed to the dime novel stage by 1947.

Stranger	"Howdy friend," he called to the Masked Rider. "I heard about you when I was down Texas way two years ago."
Masked Rider	"I call no man friend," the masked stranger answered sternly, "I take no sides, except on the side of right."

– Dialogue by Chuck Martin

The later Masked Rider stories also played down the eerie effects that Schisgall achieved in the earlier stories, perhaps the most notable thing about The Black Caballero, as he was known, and his Mexican-Indian sidekick, Blue Hawk, was the obvious resemblance to the Lone Ranger and Tonto.

The Lone Ranger Magazine ran only eight issues (April, 1937 to November, 1937) and featured a short Lone Ranger novel (no author given, but assumed to be creator Fran Striker), plus the regular pulp Western editorial chat column, "Chuck Wagon Chats" (in the last issue the editor was still soliciting, "An' if yuh ain't joined up in our *Lone Ranger*

Magazine Club yit, fill out the coupon an' send it to us, enclose a three-cent stamp an' we'll git your membership cyard out tuh yuh muy pronto, an' welcome uyh around this yere ol' chuck wagon good an' plenty friendly"). The dialect is pure Western Manhattanese; characteristic of those writers and magazines that were totally devoid of any knowledge, understanding, or experience with things Western. There was a pen-pals column, a full-page cartoon, an article about stamp or whatever collecting, a comic book type feature, an "Outdoor Trails" column, an "Interesting Facts About The West" feature, and illustrated (photos) story of a then-current Western movie, a "true" fact article such as "Famous Frontier Flights," a second comic book-type feature, and a short West-ern story. The cover art by H.J. Ward was of superior quality, and cap-tured the Lone Ranger as a tough, no-nonsense, moody personality. Ward did some excellent covers for the Spicy group (*Spicy Adventure, Detec-tive, Mystery* and *Western*), reproductions of which can be seen in Tony Goodstone's book, *The Pulps.*

The spice in *Spicy Western Stories* pales beside the open and candid scenes common in today's skin magazines, but at the time, it was "hot stuff":

> ...And the eyes of the four riders were taking in every detail of white, swelling thighs, and her tightly bound bosom as the girl's ...

or

> Inevitably, she wore silken sweaters that were cut low in front and fitted tightly, so that when their horses broke into a canter or trot, soft breasts, quivering and dancing, were enhanced by the glimmering silk that accented them.

or

> ...He felt guilty as he watched her climb into riding breeches that clung lovingly, caressingly to full hips, watched her thrust her body into a silken sweater that accented the arrogant, up-thrust beauty of her quivering breasts.

These were the sexual fantasies of the thirties and forties as interpreted by the pulp writers—lots of breast and thigh meat for the voyeuristic, and some minor sadomasochistic details tossed in for variety, all very mild stuff, mind you. Intercourse may have been circumstantially implied on occasion, but never directly (or indirectly for that matter) related. America during these years was still largely puritanical.

As with his dime novel brother, sex for the pulp Western hero was restricted to the chaste kiss. While the Western is not so staid today (indeed, the recent advent of "adult" Westerns has broken the sex barrier), Elmore Leonard's comment that men don't go to see a Western movie (or read a Western story) for sex, but for action, still largely reflects the unchanged sex habits of the Western fictional hero over the years. Such enormously popular modern Western writers as Louis L'Amour continue to produce books that scarcely mention the subject.

Robert A.W. Lowndes, editor of the Double Action Group of Western pulp magazines, and later editor of many science fiction magazines, always encouraged series characters, "The few letters we got from the readers indicated that's what they wanted." The Rio Kid was the most popular Double Action creation, making it into the hardcover as Captain Mesquite. The Silver Kid by Ford Rober (under the penname T.W. Ford) was another popular Double Action Western hero.

Sonny Tabor of *Wild West Weekly* was cast in the pattern of the "good" bad guy, *a la* Deadwood Dick:

> Wanted Sonny Tabor - $6,500 Dead or Alive. A total or more than $6,000 in rewards will be paid by Arizona Territory and various counties for the apprehension of this dangerous fugitive from justice! Officers and private citizens are urged to use the utmost caution when approaching this man, as he is known to have killed at least twenty men and has been twice condemned to death by Arizona courts.

Sonny Tabor and Pete Rice would participate in a phenomenon unique to *Wild West Weekly*—the crossover. A crossover in the parlance of the comic fan occurs when a superhero from one magazine or series makes an appearance in a story featuring another super hero. There were twenty of these crossover stories between 1933 and 1941. Each one is a prized collector's item for those whom cherish the *Wild West Weekly* brand of Western drama.

Pistol Pete Rice (in *Pete Rice Western Adventures* written by Street and Smith staff writer Ben Conlon under the house name Austin Gridly) was the sheriff of Buzzard Gap, Arizona. His adventures usually involved his deputies (Teeny Butler and Misery Hicks), his oldest friend (Sam Hollis) and his mastiff (Vulcan). In a sense, Rice was more of a modern detective than a rootin' tootin' pulp cowboy, as the crimes and circumstances surrounding them were modern and not particularly Western (e.g., counterfeiting). The only super hero devices employed by our heroes were Rice's brace of .45's, the Australian bullwhip used by Teeny Butler, and the Argentine bola used by Misery Hicks. Overall, Rice didn't do that much to stir emotions, and has been described as a tin copy of the "Man of Bronze" (Doc Savage). As with the Doc Savage pulp, the editors offered prospective members of the Pete Rice club (for .10) a deputy badge and a copy of the pledge, "As a deputy of the Pete Rice Club I pledge to at all times do my duty to my country and myself, to obey its laws, uphold its traditions, to be proud of America, and have America be proud of me!" Pete ran from November of 1933 to June of 1936 and appeared in one crossover with Sonny Tabor ("Pete Rice Rides down Sonny Tabor," *Wild West Weekly*, August 15, 1936).

The Sonny Tabor stories were written by Paul Powers using the penname Ward M. Stevens. As it turns out, Rice and Tabor are more allies than they are adversaries. Both finish the story in one piece. The cover of this particular issue is an excellent piece of pulp art that shows Rice handcuffing Tabor to a chair. The foreground shows unusual detail, and in the background, it is possible to see out of the jail window to a nighttime scene, horses, an adobe-type building, and the black night beyond. The artist, R.G. Harris, could have taken a number of short cuts, such as blacking out the outside world, but instead produced a thing of beauty. *Wild West Weekly* was one of the few Western pulp magazines to give the cover artist a credit line on the table of contents page.

W. Ryerson Johnson's Len Siringo, "a free-lance lawman," was a frontier crusader, champion of the underdog, and one of the many Doc Savage-type Western characters created by Ryerson for *Western Story* and *Star Western* over the years. Johnson was a *Western Story* regular who did these of the Doc Savage novels on the side (*Land of Always Night*, *Fantastic Island*, and a draft of *Motion Menace* that was never published). Johnson's characters in *Western Story* include Strap Masterson (R.C. Mountie), Old Pop Reeves (prospector), and Clem Hill (sheriff).

Johnson's Westerns read smoothly and easily. His dialogue was in the terse and tough *Black Mask* style:

> Quick bursts of talk, puzzled mutterings sounded above the dismal pelt of rain. The dead man slumped sideways from where he had been propped against the barrel. The rain beat on his bloated face.
>
> There were two shots, roaring six-gun detonations piled and on top of the other. This was the surprising thing. Both of the bullets went through Pinochle Hess' heart.
>
> The gun slipped from his hand into the mud. His lids fluttered vaguely over the pale eyes then his squat body, braced on feet wide apart, twisted slowly forward, falling with a kind of corkscrew motion.

Johnson was an excellent storyteller who could deliver believable action stories that relied in part upon psychological dimensions and inner motivations;

> He had moments of high exultation in which dreams of what a hundred pounds of gold could buy, banished awareness of the growing empty land with the sun continually driving splinters of fire through his brain, the high ecstatic moments became wider spaced and the hundred pound burden rode his back with grueling reality, rubbing his muscles with lightning jabs of pain.
>
> By the time he reached his first water cache, the canteen he carried was empty. He didn't let the fact alarm him. Although in making this distance before, he had used a canteen full of water, and before he had not been weighted down with gold.
>
> In blood pounding exhaustion, he lurched against the black shelving of rock, as hot to the touch as the top of a stove. Resting his pack, twisting his arms painfully out of the shoulder loops, he sank to his knees and commenced

pawing up sand in search of buried canteen.

Lethal doubts assailed him. Unreasoning doubts.

What if the canteen should be gone?

Man against nature was a frequent Johnson theme, whether it be cold ("On the opposite canyon slope the sub-artic wind, whipping down from the empty Canadian Barrens, seeped through massed spruce needles with a moan like something dying"), heat ("It was bake-oven heat poured from a glazed sky and help captive by a horizon-rimmed desolation of rock, sand, and straggly cactus"), water ("...bucking the massed ice, scraping snags of white-laced rock, there was no second when disaster did not threaten", avalanche (...in the Yukon avalanche belt 'wet slides' writhed downward, denuding whole mountain slopes and piling a giant's jumble of snow, ice, talus, and matchstick timber in the cold, shuddering valleys" or rain ("Rain beat in raw bursts over Silver Lode. Two days of it had puddle the street in front of the hitch racks and floated off sections of the wooden sidewalk.").

Johnson, like many other pulp Western fictioneers, did some fine detective stories over the years, and wound up his pulp career as editor of *New Detective*. His pulp career did not end his writing career, however. Today, Johnson works in children's stories (*Cricket Magazine*) from dual bases in Honolulu and Main, where, now in his seventies, he still practices the freelancer's art.

Probably the most enduring of all pulp Western super heroes was Zorro:

> "This confounded Zorro!" Diego's father exploded.
> "The masked highwayman who rides the hills and trails
> and says he is aiding the mistreated and oppressed." Diego
> sat up straight, his eyes met those of his father squarely, and
> a message flashed between them. For Don Diego, adjudged
> by all to be an indolent dreamer, was also Senor Zorro.

Author Johnston McCulley used the dual identity, the comic-relief sidekick, and the popular cause (an oppressed minority), all super hero theme variants, to set off Zorro, alias Don Diego Vega. Zorro started out in *Argosy*, ran in *West*, and was a popular radio and film character in the thirties (played by John Carroll and Reed Hadley), in the forties (George Turner and George Lewis), and the fifties (Ken Curtis, Richard Simmons and Clayton Moore).

The scene, first described in the pulps and later to be seen in many

Republic serials, where Zorro carves his "Z" in the belly of a fat landlord is cherished childhood memory:

> "*Dios!*" he cried. "We have been blind! Look at this fellow's wound. Do you not see, and understand? It is in the form of a ragged letter Z, is it not? 'Tis the mark of Zorro! This Don Nameless as he is called, he was Senor Zorro! We have been seen a master of fence at work— and have seen him leave his mark behind!'"

The *Zorro* of the pulps carried a subtitle" The Robin Hood of Old California and that about says it all.

A Zorro-type character (by E.B. Mann, possibly McCulley) was featured in a Grosset & Dunlap hardcover in 1936…"a mysterious bandit known as El Sombra (The Shadow) was warring on Cuesta, robbing him simply to turn over his ill-gotten gains to the small land owners." A note inside the title page states, "In its serial presentation, one of the characters in this novel appeared under a different name." El Sombra was, in reality, Senor James Bennet Sinclair, and, as the story unravels, the father's best friend of Jim Sinclair is Don Rodolfa Vega, which, I suppose, makes Zorro and El Sombra cousins. McCulley penned some excellent Westerns for *Western Story Magazine* as well. His narrative was smooth, his dialogue believable, and he combined both to tell an action-packed story with elements of humor.

The Western superhero had two strikes against him. He couldn't run around in red underwear, and he couldn't leap tall buildings or perform other super-power type acts, all of which left him at a disadvantage when competing with the emerging comic book super heroes. Other than the addition of a mask and a gimmick or two (whips were very big), the readers' credulity was never strained, nor could he ever be allowed to surrender completely his brain to his imagination. This gave the pulp Western super hero a leg up on the older adventure reading public. Some of the pulp Western heroes who achieved a super status were working cowboys, a rarity in fiction. Hopalong Cassidy appeared as a working cowboy (foreman of a bunch of line drivers) in three pulp Western magazines (Fall 1950, Winter 1951, and Spring 1951). The stories were credited to Tex Burns, a penname for Clarence Mulford, who had written the first "Hoppy" stories as early as 1910. The "Hoppy" of the pulp magazines was in the tradition of the early Mulford novels, and was not the Cassidy we saw

portrayed on TV by William Boyd. An early description by Mulford describes "Hoppy" as a scruffy, foul-talking, tobacco-chewing ranch hand. His redeeming striking personality of all the men in his outfit; humorous, courageous to the point of foolishness, eager for a fight or frolic, nonchalant when one would expect him to be quite otherwise, curious, loyal to a fault, and the best man with a Colt in the Southwest, he was a paradox and a puzzle even to his most intimate friends." In spite of all these highly admirable qualities, the pulp "Hoppy" wouldn't make it to the fourth issue; yet Bill Boyd (who won the title role in *Hopalong Cassidy* from James Gleason in 1939) would live to see the "Hoppy" character gross $70 million in 1952, at the height of the TV Western boom.

Before "Hoppy" became popular (prior to 1935), Mulford was producing prodigiously long (upwards of 75,000 words) stories for *Complete Western Book Magazine, Western Novel* and *Short Stories*.

Mulford was a down-easter (a Maine native) who wrote Westerns for nearly twenty years without ever having been West of Bangor.

Those pulps that featured strong central characters in the manner of *The Shadow* and *Doc Savage Magazine* were the bestsellers of their day, and are, today, the most collectible pulps. Other notable single-character or series-type Western pulp heroes include Chief White Eagle, which ran for three issues (October and December 1941, and February, 1942) just before the paper shortage hit; Jim Hatfield of the Texas Rangers (whose only demonstrated super talent lay in the area of gunplay); Alamo Bowie (who had an adversary with the name of Black Bart); The Silver Buck (alias Dade Solo) who rode through five issues under three titles, *Western Dime Novels, Red Star Western* and *Silver Buck Western*, with author James Olsen at the reins and finally, the dozens of "kids," most of whom never made it to the second installment.

The greatest of all pop Western super heroes nearly made it into the pulps. Harry Sinclair Drago recalls discussing the proposal for a *Tom Mix Western* pulp magazine with Mix at his home, but for one reason or another, the magazine never got financed. Too bad, this would have been a great one.

Further Variations

As with the pulp magazine in general, variety was infinite. There was a title for every possible character, subject, or mood. Most of these magazines are anonymous even to the dedicated collectors, and, in fact, there was not very much to distinguish one from another if we discount *Western Story Magazine* and *Wild West Weekly*.

There was always a close affinity between the pulp Western and the movie "B" Western; most of the "B" Westerns were in fact, based on pulp characters or situations, so it was strange to see the movies actually spawning pulps. *Movie Western* was one of at least two Western pulp magazines (the other being *Cowboy Movie Thrillers*, a Munsey magazine) that tried to cash in on the popularity of the "B" Western film, as is demonstrated in this promo piece:

> Almost everyone who likes Western stories likes Western movies, and vice versa. We thought, therefore, that we'd try to give you something you'd really like a combination of the two. We obtained the most interesting and expertly written original Western stories as we could get (at a penny a word), then, with the cooperation of the motion picture studios, we illustrated those fine stories with the most superb pictures available, using scenes from your favorite movies. (This means someone found a box of publicity stills).

Volume 1, Number 1 of *Movie Western* was published with great expectation, by Albing Publications, Jerry Albert, and Editor. The first issue

(July 1941) featured a toothy cover photo of Gene Autry, then Hollywood's number four box office draw, and sold for a mere 10 cents. While a few of the seven stories were written around one or two of the publicity stills, most of the stories had nothing whatever to do with the movies for which the stills were made. The following disclaimer appears in small print on the title page of *Movie Western*:

> Unless otherwise indicated, all stories presented here are original fiction and have no connection with any motion pictures.

In addition to the regular "departments," *Movie Western* carried two brief biographies ("The Lowdown on the Higher-ups in Western Movies") of Autry and Bill Boyd, both studio boilerplates. If this weren't enough, the fiction was terrible:

> Both of Singing Sam's six-guns were empty now and the magazine of his Winchester as well.

> The robbers had not expected action as prompt and decisive as this. They rode weary horses, and it soon became evident that the pursuers would overtake them.

The photos (with the exception of the covers) didn't reproduce well on the pulp paper. All in all, *Movie Western* would have been at most a complete bust had it not been for the interesting role it played in a wild cycle of popular culture events, Western films featuring Gene Autry and Roy Rogers in such titles as *Back in the Saddle* and *In Old Cheyenne* were written around the film's title songs, and the publicity stills from these films were give to *Movie Western* pulp writers with instructions to crank out a story around each, making certain the their stories would have "no connection with any motion picture." Understand?

The Ace High magazines of Clayton Publications were mostly Western material, and featured a complete novel, several short stories, a serial novel, and two departments, "The Sluice Box" and "The Country Store," the former being a discussion by John A. Thompson (mining expert) of questions relating to mining, and the latter being a reader swap section. The early Clayton logo, a blue flag, was changed to a blue triangle when

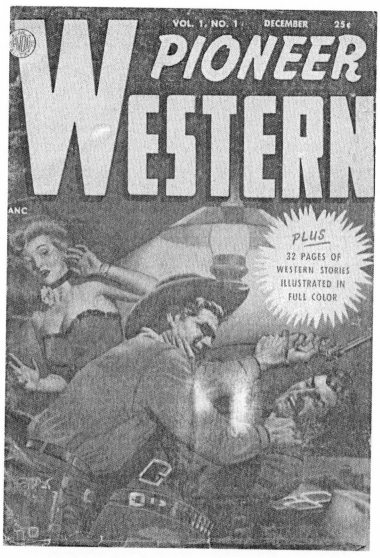

the three best Western pulp magazines were selling well (*Ace High, Cowboy Stories,* and *Ranch Romances*). After Clayton declared bankruptcy, Popular Publications picked up *Ace High* (while Street and Smith picked up its sister magazine, *Astounding*). *Ace High* employed some good writers and artists over the years, including Ray Nafziger (Robert Dale Denver), and cover artist Gerry Delano, who did some of the best interior artwork, pulp or slick, in the early *Ace Highs*. Harold Hersey attributes the initial success of *Ace High* to W. Bert Foster and his "Homer of the Lazy D" stories. Foster, a self-effacing man of many misfortunes produced Westerns for *Ace Highs and Ranch Romances* until he went completely blind.

Digest-sized Western pulp magazines were always popular. Some were designed to the 7 ½ x 5 ½ format (*Zane Grey Western*), and some (*Western Story*) evolved to that size in two or three reductions over the years, for economic reasons. A particular group of digest pulp magazines that featured novel-length stories from the pulps. These magazines didn't carry any advertising, ads, or departments and were generally advertised in the regular Western pulp magazines. Publishers included Popular Library, Readers Choice Library, and Novel Selections, Inc., and ran from the 1930's through the 1950's.

Wagon Train, perhaps the last Western pulp magazine to be newly published, was a spin-off of the TV series, which in turn could be traced back through the pulps to Emerson Hough's book, *Covered Wagon*, which was the basis for the first epic film Western.

Avon's initial success in the paperback market apparently encouraged them to try a unique approach to the Western pulp. The product was *Pioneer Western* (Vol. 1, No. 1 issued December, 1950), a 130-page comic book/pulp magazine hybrid that met no success in the marketplace. Just before the collapse of the pulp industry, Avon editor Donald A. Wollheim had planned to bring out a *Wild Bill Hickock Western*, but, like the Tom Mix magazine, it never saw print even though the first story feature, "Two for Law and Order," had been written by J. Edward Leithead.

With the exception of the top few Western pulp magazines that carried the names of three of the most proficient and widely read Western pulp writers, there wasn't much to distinguish the remainder of the Western pulp magazines. Luke Short (Fred Gidden's penname), Max Brand (one of Frederick Faust's pennames), and Walt Coburn (who had two magazines carrying his name) were three of the best containing their names. Perhaps the only other writer to deserve similar treatment was Ernest Haycox, the man Nelson Nye credits with elevating pulp Western fiction to slick status.

By the early 1950's, the sun had set on what remained of the pulp era and the writers were out trying to make it in newspapers, slicks, paperbacks, TV scripting, etc., while the few remaining editors were culling their files to produce the likes of *Top Western Fiction Annual*, a reprint magazine which was 100% old material dating back to the 1930's. The pulps were abruptly killed by their distributors; a few Western titles hung on in pulp or digest-sized magazines, but most were gone by the 1960's. Various later attempts at starting Western fiction magazines (*Zane Grey Magazine* for example, with stories written by Grey's son) were abysmal failures.

"The cowboy magazines were always the best-selling of the pulps, and they used up an enormous amount of material, from honest and authentic to false and unreal."

— Ron Goulart, *Cheap Thrills*

The Pulp Western Story

"With six-guns, horseflesh, Indians, and specialized violence ever-present, the Western is probably the most stylized dramatic form since the Greek tragedy."

— *Life Magazine*, December 20, 1963

"Two bullets through his left shoulder and two glanced off his ribs. Lost a lot of blood but he'll pull through all right."

— *Western Story Magazine*

THE WESTERN PULP STORY

The only rejection slips Frederick Faust (Max Brand) ever received from a publisher of Western fiction were for stories that committed the unspeakable crime of character development. Frank Blackwell, editor of Street and Smith's *Western Story Magazine*, returned three of Faust's stories with the statement that there was too much character development – and for the pulp Western formula he was certainly right. Blackwell, as story editor, knew the pulp Western reading public was not in the market for character development or inner motivations; he had simplified the pulp Western plot to a variety of two (1) pursuit and capture, and (2) delayed revelation and he further felt that the latter was a minor variation of the former. *Destry Rides Again* is the most famous example of plot number one and the dime novel *Seth Jones*, first and most famous of the Beadle Westerns, is the foremost example of the second.

Faust went one-step further than Blackwell did. "I've written three hundred Western books and used only one plot, the good man becomes bad and the bad man becomes good, that way you have conflict. If the bad man stays bad and the good man stays good, you have no conflict."

Frank Gruber, a contemporary of Faust and nearly as prolific writer, wrote formula. Western pulp fiction against his all-inclusive checklist of seven basic Western stories:

1. The Union Pacific Story
2. The Ranch Story
3. The Empire Story
4. The Revenge Story
5. Custer's Last Stand
6. The Outlaw Story
7. The Marshal's Story

With a Faust plot and a Gruber story, the Western pulp theme has been circumscribed. Gruber elaborates on these categories in his book *The Pulp Jungle* but the story idea of each of his categories is apparent. Gruber further rejects suggestions that any Western story could not fit his basic seven. He's probably correct since the pulp Western did not concern itself with the existential dilemma found only in the modern Western drama. So as long as the Western story was formed by the external world and further limited to action themes, the Gruber list is acceptable with some possible minor variations.

Each of Gruber's seven stories has a great potential for intra-personal hostilities, ranchers vs. the homesteaders, the marshal vs. the outlaw, the railroad vs. the landowner, the railroad vs. the landowners, cowboys vs. the Indians, and so forth. While the love story came along a little late in the pulp Western cycle, it did enjoy large sales and a long life.

The type of story that W. Ryerson Johnson did, man against the elements, does not fall neatly into the Gruber list nor does the story that traced the history of a particular gun as it passed from one user to another. A number of stories were also in the Western pulp magazines that could as easily have been set in, say, Kennybunkport, Maine, such as the Doc Swamp stories by Ben Frank in *Texas Rangers*.

Current best-selling author, Louis L'Amour, complains that when a story is set West of the Mississippi, it is classified as a Western, the implication being that it should be treated or categorized on the bases of its quality and content, not its locale. Certainly, books set east of the Mississippi are not categorized as Easterns. I can sympathize with L'Amour's point of view but I cannot ignore the fact that the term "Western" has a particular meaning for a large number of people or that it is a synonym for "cowboy pitcha", the "B" Western film. This is not a put-down as such films are entertaining and have survived many so-called quality films of their day.

In any event, the pulp Western story was an action-packed drama with lots of gunplay. It started with what was called in the trade the narrative hook, an opening sentence or paragraph to "hook" the reader's interest. From there, it followed the dictum of the pulp-detective fiction grinder, e.g., if you don't know what to do next, someone comes slamming through the door with a gun in his hand.

Allan R. Bosworth was a formula Western writer who worked the *Wild West Weekly* range for nearly 200 stories. A typical narrative book of Bosworth's:

> Captain Judson Murk of the Lost Forks Ranger Camp noticed a puffing of alkali dust indicating a man walking on foot coming north from the panhandle. Not many men walked in the area of "Cap" Murk's jurisdiction, which was all of Texas south of No Man's Land.

After the narrative hook pulled the reader into the story, it was now necessary to hold his attention:

> Deming pushed open the door to the barroom. Deming was counting on surprise but not on what broke loose when he stepped through that door. He was not counting on the violent rage that seethed up and boiled over in Ed Presley at the sight of Gore. In that second of fatal stillness, Deming's eyes caught an instantaneous flash of Sam Gore and Alf Logan, staring open-mouthed from the other end of the bar, and he faintly glimpsed the white-aproned bartender as he plunged under the counter in a crashing dive. In that same short second, without uttering a word, Ed Presley drew and fired point-blank at Sam Gore.

While the pulp story did not live by action alone, action provided 95% of the story and what little inner dialogue or personal reflection took place was sufficient for the readership:

> Ringo said no more. He thought of the man and tired-
> faced woman back on the riverbank. They would be happy
> when they learned they did not have to leave the valley.
> Many folks would be happy now, Ringo knew. He would
> ride back the way he had come, finding meager satisfac-
> tion in the knowledge that the kid wasn't going back with
> him to hang in that distant Texas town. Ringo wondered
> if he could ever forget a girl named Rose.

The best way to understand how a Western pulp story was constructed is to go back to those thrilling days of *Wild West Weekly* and ask on of the regulars how he did it. The following account of the generation of a pulp Western is reprinted here from *Writer's Digest*, March 1939.

"PLOTTING THE PULP WESTERN STORY"
by Walter A. Tompkins

The Egyptian sun had pushed the mercury to 134 in the shade that torrid April morning. I couldn't find any shade as I clambered up a gru-eling slope of the Great Pyramid with every tread of that Brobdingnagian stairway measuring three feet.

However, a reward was awaiting me at the sun-parched apex to make up for the blisters under my pith helmet and the sweat being poached on out of my skin.

Crawling at last out onto the 26-foot square summit of the Pyramid, I found a superb view toward the Sahara Desert and over the Nile Valley; a French archeologist panting there ahead of me and a plot germ for a pulp magazine cowboy story!

It was this way. The Frenchman was mumbling a platitude as we stared off through the hazy distance at the spidery minarets and gleaming mosques of Cairo:

> "This ancient Pharaoh, Cheops. He built this mighty
> pile to preserve his mummy and to make sure he could take
> his riches to Heaven with him, *n'est-ce pas*? He didn't succeed
> any better than the lowliest *Fellahin* slave buried in yon dunes."

This was a trite comment that was uttered in essentially the same terms by generations of pyramid-climbing predecessors before us. I fished a limp notebook out of sweat-sopped linens and jotted down a plot memo for future use, Write a cowboy story based on theme that a man can't take riches with him when he dies.

This Egyptian episode was back in 1934. In the interim, I returned to California and pounded out a couple of hundred Western novelettes and serials before my imaginative powers tail-spun and I had to look in my field notes for inspiration.

Fountainhead of ideas, insurance against doldrums, such is any author's notebook, his storehouse of fleeting thoughts.

Thumbing through a batch of scribbled "plot germs," I came across that forgotten notation scribbled atop a Pharaoh's tomb in remote Egypt more than four years before.

The ultimate result was in the December 17th issue of Street and Smith's *Wild West Weekly* magazine titled, tombstone Calaboose."

I started with a fresh sheet of paper in our typewriter and boiled my plot idea down to the phrase, "You can't take it with you."

That's the hackneyed bromide our plot germ boils down to, we can see at first glance. However, George Kauffman and Moss Hart fashioned an incredibly successful Broadway play out of the same theme. Frank Capra's screen version using the epigram itself for a title was a box office hit.

Surely, the theme, unoriginal and axiomatic though it is, contains meat enough for a fast action Western thriller. Fortified with the knowledge that our basic idea is not a sterile one, we light up a pipe and chew a fingernail speculatively.

"Obviously, since I must incorporate this idea into a cowboy yarn, my locale becomes the Wild West," I mused. "Now I gotta think up a situation involving typically Western characters. That'll be enough to chew on for a starter."

Just whom I pondered, could amass enough worldly goods out West to want to take them with him to the Last Roundup?

Possibly a lucky gambler in a saloon or an outlaw, dying with a sheriff's slug in his brisket, his saddlebags stuffed with the booty from a Wells Fargo stagecoach, or a desert rat whose prospecting netted him a fortune in *oro*. Possibly a ranny who cashed in on some wanted owl-hooter's boothill bounty. Maybe a rustler just paid off for a herd of stolen longhorns.

Remembering I'd used the gambler, the stagecoach bandit, and the obsequious rustler only a week past, I selected the gold prospector. We'll name him Hair-Trigger Timbell, since alliterative names stick in a reader's memory readily.

Timbell has reached the end of his rope, knows he's about to die, yet he wants to take his riches with him into eternity, justifiably loath to leave the fruits of his decades of man-killing labor grubbing quartz in the badlands to ungrateful or undeserving posterity.

Can't make him my hero because even the hero of a dime thriller has brains enough to know you can't take any *dinero* across the Big Divide. Well, the idea fits in plausibly with our desert rat. Let's make him half-loco, a common aftermath to a lifetime of solitude out in the sun-baked Western *malpais*.

Fine. We type off, Prospector is obsessed with idea to take gold dust with him in death.

He must hide the gold? Yes. Where would a loony prospector hide it so, after death, his ghost could return for it? That reminds u s, no supernatural stuff must crop up to flirt with a rejection slip. Everything must be logical, plausible.

"This prospector would want to have that gold buried with him but who'd bury an old codger with scads of yellow dust on him, worth $19 an ounce?" (Old West rates, not New Deal).

That's a sticker. Another stoking of tobacco in the old pipe and we emerge with a solution, Hair-Trigger Timbell will obtain a tombstone chiseled with his name, bore a hold in the bottom, and fill the hole with his gold-dust, later plugging it with a stone stopper that will escape detection.

After his death, sympathetic friends will bury him and naturally enough, install over his grave the tombstone he had purchased for the purpose. Nothin far-fetched about that.

At this stage of the plot, a disturbing factor appears. All we've got so far is a crack-brained character who's already dead before the story gets under way!

The postman interrupts our quandary with a letter from Ronald Oliphant, Editor of Street and Smith's veteran *Wild West Weekly* magazine. He requests a 12,000-word novelette featuring Tommy Rockford, a cowboy detective whose adventures I've been conjuring for 3W for the past seven years.

An order for a cowboy detective yarn, eh? Why not incorporate Tommy Rockford into this, "You can't take it with you" story we're struggling on? This gives us some impetus.

How could Tommy Rockford hear about Hair-Trigger Timbell's fantastic tombstone, inside of which the demented prospector is supposed to have sealed up a young fortune in gold dust?

Mmmm…Well, supposing that Timbell raved delirious gibberish before he died. Supposing he spilled his story about taking his gold dust with him into eternity but everyone believed he died broke so the tombstone was never investigated.

However, Tommy Rockford hearing the yarn believes it.

"Huh," I grunt, masticating a cuticle. "No conflict yet. No menace. Not even a villain. So far, this yarn wouldn't have the chance of a pullet in a rooster pen. You've got to have your hero bucking heavy odds in order to make a decent Western."

Well, that's simple enough to fix. Who'll our villain be? Since Tommy Rockford is a cowboy lawman, the villain can be some outlaw Rockford wants to arrest for a crime.

Supposing that this villain likewise hears the legend about Timbell's daffy idea of taking his gold to Heaven with him. The villain also thinks maybe the idea isn't so screwy after all, worth investigating.

Ah, now we see some conflict coming up pronto. An outlaw, let's give him the melodramatic name of the Border Lizard, by way of identification is after Hair-Trigger Timbell's tombstone, supposed to contain hidden gold. Tommy Rockford who is out to arrest the Border Lizard for some crime also wants to track down the incredible tombstone fable.

What was the Border Lizard's original crime? Well, let's make him a bank robber with a sinister reputation. Since we've named him the Border Lizard, that gives us our locale, the Mexican border country, about which our files are stuffed with photographs and other data.

Let's start typing the plot down on paper. We've got to invest our novelette with a Rapid-Action Opening, pulp Westerns demand lots of two-fisted action. Get your reader's interest right off the bat by actual physical conflict such as thundering gunfire of thudding fists, or else a hint of dire menace to come.

Could we open our story with a bank being robbed by this desperado villain of ours? Better yet, have Tommy Rockford himself a witness of that robbery, narrowly escaping death in it.

Bueno! Our first chapter, then will concern the Border Lizard's robbery of a cow town bank. Better make him murder the cashier (human life is cheap to a Western story scribe) to give Tommy Rockford double incentive to chase down and capture the Border Lizard.

Things are moving fast already. Out of town gallops the Border Lizard. Let's give him a couple of gun-hung henchmen so that Rockford will buck plenty tough odds. That's a pulp writer's theorem, incidentally. Pile the odds heavy against your poor protagonist. Make his future prospects look blacker than a derby hat in a coalmine at midnight.

What happens next, we inquire through the pipe smoke? Well, why not have the escaping bank robber flee into the Arizona desert, Tommy Rockford close behind. He overtakes his quarry at the waterhole, but as the Lizard's gang had been masked at the time of the bank robbery, Rockford must make sure of their identification before he shoots.

Hold on a minute, darn it. We've gotten off the track. We've got to drag in Hair-Trigger Timbell's tombstone and its gold, wherein lies the crux of the whole story, "You can't take it with you."

Why not construct a desert hotel and trading post at this waterhole? As an author, you're a deity who won't have to pay the carpenters, remember. This trading post would be a good place for Rockford and the villain to hear, simultaneously, the amazing fable of Hair-Trigger Timbell and his tombstone gold cache.

The trader who owns the oasis would be a logical man to recount the story. He makes it sound like a fairytale, but Tommy Rockford can see that the yarn has roused the interest of the three men he thinks may be the Lizard and his *ladrone* gang.

In fact, so rapt is their attention to the bartender's weird narrative of Timbell's tombstone that it gives Rockford a chance to go into their rooms to investigate. Sure enough, Rockford finds the stolen bank loot in their saddlebags.

At this point in the plot, we'd better give Rockford a severe setback. A good rule to follow is to throw your hero for a loss whenever he's made a good chunk of yardage. It builds up suspense, makes the reader groan, but read on.

What could be more logical than for the Border Lizard to surprise Rockford in the act of discovering the bank loot? The Lizard shoots Rockford, grabs the booty, and escapes.

It takes Rockford a few days to recover form his wound, during which the Lizard and his two evil compadres have vanished completely, their trail blotted out by an untimely sandstorm.

Our hero is checkmated. Very good for the plot interest, but hell on an author's imagination. What a job!

"I've got a hunch," Tommy Rockford thinks for us, "that the Border Lizard swallowed that tombstone yarn hook, line, sinker, and rowboat. I think I'll saddle up and ride to that Wyoming town where Timbell's grave is supposed to be."

Therefore, our next chapter changes scene in one swift stroke, eliminating boring details of his trip north. We find Rockford already up in Wyoming. Just to complicate the plot some more, suppose he finds Timbell's gravestone has disappeared.

What logical reason could account for this? Well, let's put the Wyoming cow town on the banks of the Yellowstone River. Supposing, in years past, that the river undermined the bluff on which the cemetery was placed, eventually destroying it. Among the graves, thus obligated was Hair-Trigger's Timbell's.

We've got to make that crucial tombstone appear in the story. Let's have Rockford find out that the town salvaged the tombstones from the doomed cemetery. What would people do with scores of tombstones thus rescued? Why not? Who's running this story?

Rockford discovers that the Wyoming cowfolk built a jail out of tombstones from the graves of long-since forgotten outlaws and hoodlums and they dubbed it, appropriately enough, their "Tombstone Calaboose."

Ah, there's a catchy title for the whole story! Short, apt, interest-compelling, and prime desiderata for a story title.

This particular tombstone, how can we identify it readily? Let's make it an unusual tombstone for a Western boot hill graveyard to boast. Supposing that Timbell, before his death, had a marble marker shipped out form Vermont, carved his name on it, and (according to the legend) this marble stone contains a secret interior compartment in which old Hair-Trigger stored his gold dust.

At this point, the villains should reappear. How to weld them into the plot plausibly will take some thought. All of this plotting has taken two or three hard hours of concentration. We find our mental forces fagged out.

I have a habit when my brain hits an impasse to simply knock off work. Play nine holes of golf or woo some music out of a marimba that I keep in my office, anything at all so long as you completely forget about your plot.

Your subconscious mind works while you are thus relaxing and ten chances to one, when you return to your desk, knots will unravel with gratifying ease.

It always works for me. I find that during my mental absence, Tommy Rockford has visited the jail-keeper of the Tombstone Calaboose and gets permission to visit the jail on the morrow and investigate Timbell's marble gravestone.

The jailer is murdered mysteriously and just to make Rockford's lot harder than it is, we'll say that the Wyoming sheriff jails Rockford in the Tombstone Calaboose, accused of the jailer's murder. All seems hopelessly lost.

When night comes, three prowlers visit the jail with chisel, block and tackle, and crowbars. They are the Border lizard and his two crooked padres who've ridden from Arizona to check up on the crazy yarn they'd heard down in the desert oasis.

The Border Lizard identifies "Timbell's gravestone because it's the only marble stone in the jail's wall (see the reason for the unusual tombstone now?). They gouge out a hole in the jail, which they believe is unoccupied.

The hole left in the jail wall enables Tommy Rockford to escape. He obtains guns and has a shoot-out with the Border Lizard and his two gunhawks, killing all three in a thrill-packed climax.

As a surprise twist in the denouement, Rockford breaks open the marble tombstone and to his astonishment, finds that Timbell didn't die broke after all. A drilled-out hold in the marble slab contains several pokes of gold dust, thereby, confirming the yarn most men figured was a figment of Timbell's deranged brain.

There *amigos* is our story, roughly sketched. Now for the actual writing. My own personal technique involved the construction of a very handy device, a brief synopsis outlined by chapters.

The reason for this is to keep the plot thread in view at all times and to make sure I don't over write a scene and have to prune it later, the latter being agonizing surgery. From long habit, I know that I must allow five 300-word pages to a chapter.

Therefore, on a single sheet of paper, I type out my telegraphic synopsis thusly, and hang it above my desk as a guide when I start composing.

TOMBSTONE CALABOOSE

Hero Tommy Rockford is in a border town bank when it is held up by a notorious killer, Border Lizard, and two masked pards. He gives chase to avenge cashier's murder and recover loot.

Rockford overtakes trio at desert oasis but isn't sure they are men he wants. Bartender recounts weird legend of a Wyoming prospector who wanted to take gold dust with him after death, so stored it in his tombstone.

This story fascinates the three visitors. While they are listening, Rockford searches their room. Just as he discovers bank loot, Border Lizard surprised him, starts shooting.

Rockford is wounded. Lizard and men get away. Rockford recovers, has only one clue to follow up. Possibly Lizard will go to Wyoming cow town to investigate story of tombstone gold cache.

Rockford arrives in Wyoming town, finds Timbell's tomb now part of jail wall. Leaving jailer's home at night, accidentally leaves hat behind. Soon after Border Lizard forces hailer to reveal location of tombstone, then kills jailer when he recognizes the gang as wanted men.

Wyoming sheriff coming to visit jailer finds him dead, discovers hat with initials "TR" in band. Rockford returns for hat and is arrested and jailed, charged with murder.

At midnight, Rockford sees mysterious trio of riders come to jail they suppose empty. With block and tackle, they remove Timbell's tombstone. Rockford crawls out hole thus made in jail wall but is surprised by sheriff.

Rockford overcomes sheriff, borrows his six-gun, kills Border Lizard and his men. Better leave one outlaw alive to corroborate Rockford and clear him with sheriff. Rockford finds gold in Timbell's tombstone thereby, bearing out story's theme of "You can't take it with you."

There you have the working outline. I make a similar one for every story I write, be it a book length serial or a short. The method works fine with me and I pass it on for what it may be worth to *Writer's Digest's* aspiring Western authors.

The published story, as you can read it in *Wild West Weekly* magazine for December 17, may seem a far cry indeed from a Frenchman's muttered comment atop the Great Pyramid in Egypt. It goes to prove that one can never tell what vagrant idea may give you the nucleus for a thrilling pulp fiction yarn. Come to think of it, there may be some occult psychic connection between the big Egyptian tomb and the title of my story laid in Wyoming, "Tombstone Calaboose." *Quien sabe?*

Today Tompkins' comments, "Took men many years to write simply and clearly without a lot of smart-ass big words." Tompkins sold his first Western novel at age 21 to *Wild West Weekly* and for the following 25 years wrote for the Western pulps under his own name, as well as the house names Philip F. Deere and Jackson Cole, and did the Ozar the Aztec series for Top Notch under the penname Valentine Wood. Today, he is a staff historian for the *Santa Barbara News Press* and has been honored by the California legislature for his "outstanding contribution to the Santa Barbara community and for his efforts in highlighting the colorful history of the Santa Barbara area."

Other Writing Techniques

Some of the old Western pulp fictioneers still active in the Western fiction business describe their techniques for crafting Western fiction:

"I always tried to create my yarns out of basically real situations, but making everything larger than life, and strictly entertainment oriented"

— Billy Burchardt

"...same as a writer in any category, I used a professional approach, planning, thinking, doodling out preliminary form and characters as needed to fit, or else starting with character idea and developing plot and action to fit him"

— C.S. Boyles, Jr.

"I'm sure some pulp writers wrote entirely from imagination and without any real knowledge of the West, but most of the good ones were working on solid ground. There was a discipline in writing for the pulps; a good story had to have good, steady movement. Characterization had to be strong, but you could seldom get away with the anti-hero types so prevalent today. Your main character in the pulps had to be pure in heart and motive, and steadfast in the face of danger. The James Garner type of reluctant hero would get you a rejection slip and the Clint Eastwood anti-hero was poison.

Some writers, and I include myself, try often to build a story around authentic history and give the reader some insight into a real time, place, or situation. We often try to put across a theme or a viewpoint, perhaps paralleling a historical situation with a present-day situation or problem. We attempted to do it subtly, however, and tried never to beat the reader over the head with it, for realized that his main interest was entertainment. If he wanted straight history, he would have gone to a nonfiction book rather than to a short story or novel. We tried to give him history and reality as a bonus"

– Elmer Kelton

Louis L'Amour, probably the best-selling living Western author, wrote a number of Western, mystery, air, adventure, and sport stories in the pulps (L'Amour himself had 54 amateur boxing fight stories he wrote), but the Western proved to be his métier:

"Probably I sold in the neighborhood of 150-200 stories of the West to the pulp magazines. I know that in one year I sold 33 stories, most of them Western. I did read the pulps, but none of the pulp writers influenced me more than any other did. Writing for the pulps did have an influence, and that was their requirement that one have a story to tell and that it must move."

L'Amour's observations ring true, the good Western pulp was a well-told tale with plenty of action. Why then were such yarns popular in a period of serious national economic distress? Some of the old-timers who offered their views think that the Western protagonist of the time had yet to be replaced by sports, military, and aviation heroes, and the early 1930's were not that far removed from the Western expansion movement.

Perhaps the Western pulp story was popular because it told a heroic tale of a single man up against the hostile odds of his environment, certainly a theme the male of the depression years could readily identify and sympathize with. The reader could vicariously work through complicated sets of personal problems he faced in the real world as well as immerse himself in an action-packed yarn. So on both the symbolic and realistic levels, the

Western pulp story had something good to offer readers, something cathartic. The depression was tough on writers as well as readers:

> "The depression made quitters out of a lot of people, particularly the spoiled boys who thought they were extra special, but weren't. Rates fell way down, but there was always a market somewhere if you had guts enough to stick it out and keep on plugging. Those tough years were the best training in the world, a man found out what his real capacity was"
>
> – L.P. Holmes

If you read a few pulp Westerns from each decade since the 1920's, you will note that the quality of the writing has improved, that the characters are more believable, the dialogue no longer archaic, and something is finally being done with character development. Certainly, no one today is writing Western fiction that is not steeped in the history of the time and circumstances surrounding his fiction.

> "I think Westerns will continue to be popular, though on a more selective basis now because they're gusty. Hard men living hard times, and the exception of death is always right around the corner. You can tell any kind of a story you want against a Western background, but there is always the expectation that sooner or later, the guns are going to go off. Leather, sweat, raw, whisky, and gunfire, put some girls in if you want, but people don't go to a Western movie to see the girls, they go to see the guns go off and get a vicarious kick out of it and leave the theatre lighting a cigarette the way the hero did. The guns went off louder than they ever did before in *Shane*, reached a peak in *The Wild Ones* and now we're regrouping to see if there are any other ways to do it, to keep Westerns fresh and interesting:
>
> – Elmore Leonard

"I would be perfectly happy if I never had to read another Western"
— Robert A.W. Lowndes, Editor of the Double Action Group

The Men Behind the Mask—
The Editors

"When the thing finally collapsed, the publishers blamed the editors, who in turn blamed the writers, and the only thing they could do was go home and kick their wives"
— Tom Curry talking about Ned Pines (Popular Publications) and Leo Margulies (Editor of the Thrilling Group).

The Western pulp editor's lot was not a happy one. Torn between the pressures of getting a half doze or so magazines out on the street to meet a newsstand deadline, and developing and nurturing a cadre of writers on the other hand, he more often than not botched both jobs.

There was not a great lasting relationship between Western pulp editors and writers, nor between these editors and the readers, so is it not surprising to discover that the Western pulp genre produced no John W. Campbells or Farnsworth Wrights.

I've talked with Western pulp editors who told me that, in many cases, they didn't' even have time to read a story before plugging it into publication in order to meet some close deadline, and I've talked to writers who swear that were it not for an editor's interest in his work, he'd never have made it. Therefore, while the bulk of Western writers/readers/editors enjoyed an anonymous relationship, there were significant variations at both ends of the spectrum.

I have a note from the late Graves Gladney (a pulp artist who did a few Western covers), who stated, "I should have told Steeger to go fuck himself and then knocked the B-Jesus out of him. I could have don't it then and I damn sure could do it now."

For contrast, I offer the following five-page rejection letter sent to Elmore Leonard from Popular editor Mike Tilden, used with Leonard's kind permission:

"LETTER FROM THE EDITOR,"
BY MICHAEL TILDEN

Popular Publications, Inc.
November 21, 1951
205 East 42nd Street
New York, 17, NY

Dear Dutch:

I want to thank you very much for your letter of October 29, and for your stories.

By all means, keep on speaking freely to me, or to any other editor. That is one of the nice things about this business. The friendships, even though they are via remote control, that you pick up and the regard (with), which the editor holds these friends as writers. God knows it isn't the dough connected with a job like this!

I wish I could tell you the difference between a slick pulp story, outside of the very obvious factors, which you know yourself. Of course, the first thing, again to be obvious, is the fact that pulp stories, as a general rule, and with the notable exception of *Adventure* and *Blue Book*, are all categorized, if there is such a word, by the magazine *Western Stories, Love Stories, Detective Stories*, etc. But within those limits, again, what is the difference between a good Western story, which I would run, and one that's an *SEP (Saturday Evening Post?)* acceptance?

The chances are, again, in a good Western story, I would take anything that *The Post* or *Collier's* would run, depending upon length, of course, and I'd use it with a good deal of pleasure. For various reasons, including that intangible thing called "slant," they might turn down any number of otherwise good stories. There are several things to account for this.

One is that their fiction is pretty well limited (in quantity). (The market)…is much more competitive than ours is, as you can see by looking at the table of contents in any of those magazines. They don't have a great deal of room for their fiction. And of course, there is the advertising setup to be taken into consideration. That doesn't bother us nearly as much, since we are almost entirely dependent upon newsstand sales, to the extent, our yardstick in judging fiction is generally much more elastic. I think that both the big magazines and we like stories that give the reader some kind of lift. Overpriced as our magazines are, we assume none of those readers wants to shoot a quarter to get a story that ends on a downbeat, a frustrated, or an indeterminate ending. After all, our customers are buying entertainment, and it is our job to give it to them.

I wouldn't say that there is very much difference in structure between a good pulp and a good smooth paper story. I will take, and have taken, stories, which I think are pretty good, but in which I was not too well satisfied with the structural balance of the story, and the treatment of characterization, some of which are not followed through as well as I would have wished, and which quite probably, other things being equal, could well have accounted for a smooth paper rejection. Characterization, of course, is of primary importance in any story, which means being sure to follow through with your character, making him stand for something, mean something, and yet not digress from the ground rules governing his behavior, which you have already laid down.

Motive, again, is sometimes slighted in pulp; sometimes it's rather complex or rather hazy. This I think, is bad in any story, for the motive, the reason why of the character's thought and action, should be absolutely credible, basic in its simplicity, and so natural that there is never any shadow of doubt in the reader's mind as to why one character behaves as he does. And the smooth paper boys are keen to spot a sour or inadequate motive.

The pulps have for a long time gone in, I think unadvisedly, for outlandish words and expressions. That is, Western cowboy slang, either genuine or ersatz and if the story is laid down around the Border, a lot of Mexican words and expressions get in, under the writer's impression that it makes for color and verisimilitude. I have known cases where stories, which were possible acceptances by smooth paper magazines, were turned down simply because of this. The reader simply didn't understand what all these Mexican italicized words and expressions mean, or what the word "soogans" or "quirly," etc., would mean in a Western. And I think too, that they've been vastly overdone.

Some years ago, we went to vast expense and some trouble to get a reader survey. Since this by now is pretty well obsolete, and since it did practically nothing useful, I'd just as soon tell you very roughly what we found about our audience. We found that the typical reader was a young man about in his middle 20's, who had a couple of years into high school, was employed, usually by some large organization in some job in which he used his hands pretty much. He had a wife and one and a fraction children, a small amount of money in the bank, a second-hand car, and hoped to own his own house.

I don't know what good that would do you toward answering your question, but it's a safe bet that this type of magazine seems to sell pretty well in manufacturing towns, rather than in the major cosmopolitan centers.

Precisely what slanting is, I really don't know. It is undoubtedly in the particular kind of treatment, and it has long been almost axiomatic, for example, that a story aimed for *The Post* would never go in *Collier's*, and vice versa. However, I have known several exceptions to that. I think you might be able to get a clearer picture of slant by a thorough reading of *The Post* fiction, as against *Colliers*, as against *Cosmopolitan*, or by comparing the material in *The American Magazine* fiction and that of *Red Book*, as well as others, which apparently go after more or less that same audience. The behavior of characters in their relationships, particularly men and women characters, have a good deal to do with it, I suppose, and the treatment and delineation of such characters.

The emphasis on the various fiction values is probably slightly different, also, I suppose. And "tone", some seem to go in for the light touch, some for the more serious, is another difference.

For my part, I am glad that you have chosen Westerns. That *Arizona Highways* is a great job, and you have made excellent use of it, I think in your stories. And, may I say that you must have done a powerful lot of looking in that hour you spent in Phoenix.

I am glad you like Frank Bonham's stuff. Aside from the fact that it is a good friend of mine, I have a great deal of respect for him as a craftsman. Up till the time he hit *The Post*, I ran his stories frequently to *Dime Western*. For his sake, I hope that he continues to hit *The Post* but for the sake of my magazines, I wish him all the ill luck in the world, so that I may pick up some of his stories.

Now about your story, "For Five a Day," I am especially sorry that it has to go back, because I am not quite sure just what you are getting at. If it is the irony of the more or less plodding job of being a scout, for five dollars a day, against the one day of drama of life and death, love and stuff, I think it's a little bit weak, and it is not nearly sufficiently pointed up.

There is one serious fault in here, which you might want to look out for in the future. You have not played fair with the reader. The reader has every right to suspect that the woman, as you have indicated, was the wife of finance of that passenger in the state, and yet, the reader has no inkling until the very last paragraph that she was Simon's wife. Simon knew it. The story is told through his viewpoint, and if the reader is, in a sense, in Simon's skin, the reader should know it as soon as he discovers it. There is no reason to slide over the shocking effect of her discovery on Simon. We do not know what their relationship actually was.

Maybe he didn't want her to come out, either because it was too risky or because they had distinctly fallen out of love. Maybe he was determined to have her come out because he genuinely loves her and misses her. Simon simply doesn't emerge as a real person because you have not let him do so. Even with a repressed and rather flinty character, it seems to me that the reader has a right to know a little bit more about Simon, if he is going to carry the ball. In fact, *that* actually is your story.

One other thing. I don't quite understand why he could be so silly as not to see that he was not well supplied with cartridges when he left his horse. He was a man of vast experience and knowledge at his rather grim trade, and surely the fact that he didn't bring sufficient shells with him could only be accounted for by something abnormal in his behavior or though processes. IF it was the fact of his wife's near murder, there again, the reader should know. It's a difficult problem to handle properly.

This Mata Lobo was, I though, very well done, and the scene of his stalking a stagecoach was a honey. I'll hazard a guess that he was based on the Apache Kid, although I may be wrong, of course.

I think if you want to redo this, it would be perfectly all right, except that you have given such a superficial portrait of the scout that he missed the story completely. There could be a good story written with what you have, but it would be the story, again, of this rugged, silent plains wise man that is used to looking on death and all its more horrid forms apparently without any real effect upon him. Then your story would be, did this man, for all his appearance, have nothing but ice water in his veins, feel any emotions common to his weaker, softer brothers? What would break him down into showing some humanity? Here, then, is the story of the time when he broke.

That suggestion is, or course, in an extremely rough and generalized form. It needs thinking over. It needs handling through specific incidents, and a thorough delineation of this man's character, which would have to be shown by incidents of mounting dramatic intensity until the story is complete.

If you don't wish to do this, or if the idea leaves you rather cold, by all means drop it. Perhaps, you would rather put this on the shelf, and work on something else. That, of course, is up to you. As it stands, it appears to me a story, which is not finished and not completely or definitely thought out.

I know how tough this having a job and writing at night is, and I want to tell you how much admiration I have for you, especially since I think you have a genuine talent and have shown me some really swell stuff. I know full well what that salary check means, particularly with a family to support. And fiction writing, since it is so highly competitive, seems an awfully chancy thing until you get at least a good backlog or financial reserve to tide you over the inevitable dry spells.

There is always the really horrible fate, where you find yourself on a sort of a treadmill, and just have to grind out stuff, which you are not particularly interested in, in order to get a check. That, I think, is death to an essentially creative and talented man. I would much rather see somebody not write so much, but do a conscientious job of craftsmanship than I would have somebody turn out stories, which are pure hack-adequate things, which may be publishable, but which offer absolutely no future for the writer.

Let met implore you to guard with the zeal of an 1840 model virgin protecting her fair name, your sensitivity and insight into people, and your sense and need of communication a story, because it means something to you, and you must impress its entertainment and emotional values on the reader. Don't lose it, even if you have to keep on at a job the rest of your life, and write when and as you can.

Yes, the twenty-five thousand-word deal is undoubtedly a risk of tying up that much time and effort. Unless you want to use that as sort of a jump-off, to be later incorporated in a novel. Some writers have done that with a fair amount of success, but they have been fairly well seasoned in this impossible, maddening, and utterly fascinating form of endeavor.

Regarding world length, I don't think it is a good idea to hold you down unnecessarily, but a hundred dollars is my top for short stories for five-thousand words or over. I cant' pay any more on account of budgetary considerations, and also, I find that this is inclined to act as a brake, because a short story that cannot be told in five-thousand words, I don't believe can be written at all. Also, anything over that length is a tough job to fit in mechanically in any of these magazines. And I think that you will find that the four to five-thousand-word lengths is also best suited to smooth paper, short story markets.

My length upward from five-thousand is the seventy-five to eighty-five hundred short novelettes, which, of course, becomes a novelette and not a short story. That is, there are usually more characters and it offers a larger scope in time and place. As a general rule, the focus is not quite as close- up, we get more of a panoramic view than the candid camera shot.

Again, I want to tell you how much I appreciate both your stories and your letter, and please feel free to write me at any time.

I am sorry to have to send back your story, of course, and hope that you will replace it soon with another. A happy Thanksgiving to you and your family, and let me hear from you.

Michael Tilden, Managing Editor

This letter was by no means a typical correspondence, but does reveal that sensitive, intelligent human beings do manage, on occasion, to get into positions of authority.

Bill Cox, thoroughly enjoyed his relationship with Rogers Terrill (Popular), and many of the writers I've interviewed talk fondly of their old editors, names like Don Ward, Jim Hendrix, Jr., Malcolm Reiss, Daisy Bacon, Fanny Ellsworth, and Dorothy Hubbard are mentioned fondly and frequently. Walt Coburn credits editors Jack Kelly (Fiction House), Rogers Terrill, and Harry Widner with much of his success as a writer.

Bob Lowndes edited several Western magazines and a number of others:

> I edited Westerns, detective, sports, science fiction, love, and air war pulp that folded during the 1943 paper shortage. I edited the first *Double Action Western, Famous Western Real Western Blue Ribbon Western Complete Cow-*

boy Novel, Action Packed Western, Smashing Western, Western Yarns (didn't survive the war), and *Complete Cowboy Wild Western Stories.*

I always encouraged series-type characters such as T.W. Ford's (Ford Rober) The Silver Kid. Anthony Rud had a good series and we used a lot of the Archie Jocelyn's stuff. The cover artists were H.W. Scott and A. Leslie Ross, a pupil of Scotties. Milton Luros was another. He's been in California since the pulp days.

My only hard and fast policy that affected writers was that all races had to be heroes/villains in equal proportions.

My biggest problem as an editor was getting the six to eight magazines out every month and trying to get the time to look over manuscripts.

Perhaps the most famous encounter between a Western pulp writer and his editor was when young Frederick Faust and Robert H. Davis, chief executive of Frank Munsey's publishing empire, met early in 1917. Davis prided himself on being able to spot a comer (he had purchased some of Joseph Conrad's early work, and is credited by some sources with discovering O. Henry. This is dubious, however, as Arthur Grissom, *Smart Set's* first editor, purchased O. Henry's first four stories, which were reputed to have been rejected by every magazine in the country). Editor David gave Faust the outline of a plot and told him to go down the hall where there was a small room with a typewriter, and build a story form it. Faust cranked out a 7,800-word story and returned same to Davis within two hours. Davis, amazed at Faust's speed, asked where he had learned to write. Faust's reply was, "Down the hall." The story was published in the March 1917 *All Story Weekly,* without a change.

"Heinie had trained himself to do it. Fourteen pages a day, come rain, come shine, come mood or no, Heinie wrote the fourteen pages."
  – Frank Gruber talking about Frederick Faust in *The Pulp Jungle*

Hacking Them Out
By the Dozens—
The Writers

"I was happily surprised to discover that the West was pretty much as I had imagined it and written about it"
  – Harry Wilkinson, Western pulp writer

"You should have seen him brining out the (Western) stories from his briefcase...talking to the editors like he was selling shoe polish"
  – Harry Sinclair Drago talking about Frank Gruber
    – "But his detective stories were O.K."

At one time or another, every pulp pro did a Western: Edgar Rice Burroughs, William Hope Hodgson, Erle Stanley Gardner, and Robert E. Howard are a few of the more famous pulp writers who turned out a Western or two. Although these men wrote quality Western stories, they qualify by no stretchy of the imagination as Western pulp writers.

Burroughs wrote (among others) two highly praised Westerns dealing evenhandedly and from personal experience with the Apache, and Howard, more noted for his Sword-and-Socery fiction, wrote some twenty-five Pecos Bill-type Westerns about a "gent" named Breckenridge Elkins, five humorous first-person Westerns reminiscent of O. Henry, and eleven others, including one, which I consider near perfect—*The Vultures. The Vulture's* only shortcoming is in development of characters, but as Faust and the other Western pros knew, editors were simply not in the market for this commodity. This story, reprinted in recent years by Fictioneer Books, could make one of the best film Westerns of all times. L. Sprague de Camp's biography of Howard states that he had decided at the end of his life to write only Westerns. Those Westerns Howard did complete showed the master touch.

But Howard was not a Western fiction writer. The Western pulp wordsmith was one who wrote mainly for, and earned his reputation and bread and butter in, the various Western pulp magazines.

The writers of pulp Western fiction were legion, and as pointed out earlier, the volume of stories being produced made it barely possible for editors to read all of the stories they passed along to the compositor. Out of this blur of hundreds of Western pulp magazines and thousands of writers, some distinct period in the relatively short-lived history of the Western pulp magazine can be identified, as can some distinctive writers.

The early period of Western pulp fiction was marked by a few greats such as Frederick Faust and Fred Glidden working for the variety pulp magazines such as *Everybody's* and *Popular Fiction*, and covered roughly the first twenty-0five years of the 20th century. The most significant event in terms of shaping the course of Western function during this period did not occur within pulp covers, however. Owen Wister's principle character in *The Virginian* would influence all Western fiction for years to come. "The Virginian," as interpreted by Gary Cooper, was the prototype Western fiction hero, soft-spoken but tough ("Smile when you say that"), he reinforced the Deadwood Dick character, and redefined it in terms of the (then) present.

The middle period of the Golden Age of Western pulp fiction, which featured the development and proliferation of the all-Western pulp magazine, ran from the mid-1920's to the mid-1940's, and was characterized by a handful of pros such as Tuttle, Faust, Coburn, Raine, and Drago, all of whom were turning out good Western fiction, that is, stories that were exciting reading written by the hand of a man who has had some experience with things Western. This middle period was also marked by an army of amateurs who could neither tell an exciting or authentic Western yarn, or know one if they saw on. These "writers" had learned the formula and were mechanically cranking out uninspired dribble.

Two great names to emerge from this period were H. Bedford-Jones and Ernest Haycox. While Bedford-Jones is rarely given the credit he deserves in the chronology of Western fiction, Haycox has been roundly recognized by historians for his contributions. Bedford-Jones refined the historical Western told on a grand scale against a panoramic background.

Haycox would bring the hero concept into the present decade of the twentieth century, and make the Western story not only suitable for film, but make it a so-called "star vehicle" for "name" Hollywood actors and actresses. While Bedford-Jones raised the Western to epic proportions, Haycox added some dimensions to the characters, and played with basic modifications in the Western formula. Both were successful in producing quality Western yarns.

The third and declining pulp period, which was marked by the rise of romantic themes, ran from the mid-1940's to about 1960, and would produce some writers of skill and influence who would continue their popularity beyond the pulp years and pulp magazines. Writers such as L'Amour, Omar Barker, Wayne D. Overholser, and Lewis B. Patten, had learned their skills in the Western pulp magazines, but were able to refine their abilities, find new themes, and treat old subjects in fresh ways, thereby, continuing their writing into the paperbacks after the pulp markets abruptly crashed.

The post pulp era is characterized by paperback books, some of which are being newly written by those who had labored in the pulp vineyards in the later years, and some, which are, surprisingly enough reprints of old pulp yarns, Faust's *Singing Guns*, for example has over 1.5 million copies in print. Many of the old pulp word wranglers have lived to see their yarns translated onto film, not to mention into Italian, Norwegian, German, and other languages.

Because the Western pulp story was written against a standard formula, we do find a certain uniformity of plot and many style similarities, but there were sufficient variations in the men who wrote these stories and in the stories themselves, to make for some critical comparisons.

The bulk of the pulp Western stories were mass-produced pap, the best thing that can be said for them is that they provided a source of mass entertainment. Many of the writers who worked these magazines knew nothing of the West. Rex Bundy, recent President of the Western Historical Research Associates, says that it was easy to write in this manner at one time but because of advances in communications and transportation, we are now all more sophisticated and knowledgeable, about not only our own country, but also the World at large. Bundy recalls once reading a pulp Western where the author put wings on a coyote and legs on a buzzard (attributed to John Creasey when he was working the pulp Westerns as Ken Ranger, William K. Reilly, and Tex Reilly). Richard Hill Wilkinson, a Western pulp writer with over seventy-five stories to his credit, had never been West of the Hudson River himself, and recalls a pulp Western by a fellow writer in which Doc Holliday (whom every fan of the West knows was a dentist) performed an emergency appendectomy on a saloon pool table, neither writer nor editor of his Western background "research" in New York's movie theatres. During the proliferation of the Western pulp magazine, the errors, misconceptions, and inaccuracies reached epidemic proportions, infecting all material dealing with the West to the extent that one could only read these tales as pure entertainment fiction. One gets an idea of the magnitude of the problem from scanning Ramon F. Adam's book, *A Second Look at Books and Histories of the West*. This book provides 622 double-column pages listing errors commonly found in Western fact and fiction books.

Taken as straight fiction, however, the pulp Western had a charm born of the great energy of an emerging cottage industry, and would achieve a popularity unmatched in the history of mass-produced fiction. The principal moving force in the first and second Western pulp periods was Frederick Faust. Over a twenty-year period he is credited with an output in excess of thirty million words, most of it Western material, although he also wrote fantasy adventure, historicals, and love stories. His pulp Westerns, published originally in argosy, *All Story Weekly Adventure, Argosy-All Story Weekly, Blue Book, Complete Western Book, Dime Western, Far West Illustrated, Munsey Magazine, Short Stories, Star Western, West Magazine,* and *Western Story Magazine* have had new life in paperback form, mainly under his Max Brand and Evan Evans pseudonyms: "new" books (those never before published in book form) by Faust are still being issued once or twice a year.

Faust biographer Robert Easton profiles Faust the writer; "In Faust's hands, on a good day, the pulp Western came alive with king-sized heroes in pursuit of epic-proportion bad men, against a landscape of mythological dimensions, all of it elevated by a distinctive action tone." It was just such good days that Faust, as Max Brand, produced *Twelve Peers* for *Western Story Magazine* (began February, 1930). Later printed and filmed as *Destry Rides Again* (Hollywood didn't follow Faust's story, however) it ranked with Zane Grey's *Nevada* and Jack Shafer's *Shane* as one of the great pieces of Western fiction. In hard- and soft-cover editions, *Destry* has sold well over a million copies, and was three times produced as a film; in 1932 featuring Tom Mix, in 1939 featuring James Steward (who by this time had a lock on the stereotyped Western hero) and Marlene Dietrich, and again in 1954 featuring Audie Murphy.

After a rather stormy childhood and college years in California, Faust drifted to New York where he gained the famous "...down the hall" interview with Robert H. Davis, Frank Munsey's chief executive. After an immediate success in breaking into the Munsey chain, Faust went on to produce large quantities of Western pulp fiction over the next twenty-seven years, until his untimely death in 1944, when, as a war correspondent attached to an American rifle platoon, he caught a German shell fragment in the chest during an attack on Santa Maria Infante.

In addition to his pulp fiction (of which he was not especially proud) Faust produced fiction and poetry for a variety of slicks, including *Esquire*, *Cosmopolitan* (the first and subsequent Dr. Kildare stories), *The Saturday Evening Post*, *Collier's Liberty*, *Country Gentleman*, *The Delineator*, *Pictorial Review*, *McCall's*, *Ladies Home Journal*, *Harper's*, *The Forum*, and *This Week*. In 1922, Faust wrote *The Village Street*, and in 1931, *Dionysus in Hades*, two small volumes of poetry, which he particularly liked.

In the past twenty-five years, twenty million copies of his stories have been sold in the United States, and many millions more abroad, the most popular of which are: *The Untamed, Singing Guns, Fightin' Fool,* and *The Border Kid.* Most of Faust's works were solo efforts, although he had collaborated on occasion with John Schoolcraft, Kenneth Perkins, Robert Simpson, and perhaps a few others.

After a period spent in an Italian Villa near Florence (Villa Pazzi), on the south side of the Arno River, Faust felt out of touch, and by early January 1938, was in Hollywood writing scripts at $1,500 per week. An interesting parallel occurs at this time. In July of 1939, Faust had concluded a deal worth $5,000, by which he undertook to write a film story based on James Fenimore Cooper's novel, *The Deerslayer,* for Gene Towne, an RKO producer, in thirty days. Faust and Cooper had written extensively of the Western frontier when each was in Europe, and both Faust and Cooper had done some of their best work at the John Jay estate at Katonah (Westchester, New York). Cooper completed *The Spy* on the front porch where Faust had worked on Cooper's *The Deerslayer.*

Faust, meanwhile, also returned to the pulps, service Street and Smith editor Frank Blackwell well, almost single-handedly driving *Western Story Magazine's* circulation over the million mark through the 1930s and into the 1940s. By this time, Faust had established himself as a major source of material for the film industry.

Faust's popularity can be attributed to two factors; he told a straight action story, and his imagery was clear and exciting:

> Two guns flashed like fine blue fire into the hands of Calico. The left gun he held a bit out to the side. The right gun he carried just above the height of the pommel of his saddle and flicked the hammer so rapidly with his thumb that the five shots blended into one thunder roll.

Faust could also be expansive:

> Flame rolled in a broad river up out of the Eastern sky,

or moodily introspective:

> It is something that slides in through the eyes, as music flows through the ears. One evening, the skies open and you can ride straight on into the brightness of the heavens; and all other evenings only serve to make you feel the black rim of the earth and the narrow round of it, and the long, long, long darkness.

He could be brutal:

> Blood was bursting through the fingers of his hands and streaming down over his clothes. Blondy went to him and pulled the hands away from that frightful face. He had been shot through both cheeks. When he tried to speak, blood and shattered teeth spouted out and fell on the floor.

Yet, on occasion, romantic:

> Something darkened his eyes. He looked up to the face of the girl between him and the window. The soft blue of the sky closed in about her head. There would be no end to the joy of beholding her.

Faust was one of the few Western writers with a following going beyond the pulp era, and the only Western pulp writer to enjoy a fanzine and hard core of devotees. Headed by Darrell C. Richardson and William F. Nolan, and recorded by *The Fabulous Faust Fanzine*, the Faust cult ran strong into the 1950s and 1960s, and a full two decades after Faust's death. *The Fabulous Faust Fanzine* used some early college material of Faust's, some poetry, short reviews, biographical material, and some awesome statistics:

> From 1918 to 1935, he had chalked up an average of one full-length Western novel every month for sixteen years. *Dust Across the Range*, his last Western, appeared in 1938 and was semi-modern. Only seven of his one hundred and thirty-five Western serials ever appeared in magazines other then *Western Story* and *Argosy*. In all, Faust's total Western wordage is equal to some 215 book-length novels.

Faust stories were in the hundreds; he can be identified with more than seventy films released over a period of forty years; radio broadcast based on Faust's works ran in the 1930s, 1940s and 1950s. His Westerns were produced on the stage and on television. Almost forty years after his death, he maintains an active readership. Truly, Faust was King of Western pulp genre.

Walt Coburn was one of a few bona westerners to write Western fiction for the pulps. At the peak of his forty-year career (1930s and 1940s), he produced in excess of 600,000 word search year, all of them were published, a feat that certainly ranks Coburn with Faust as one of the Western pulp big guns. Like Faust, Coburn enjoyed the grape: "John Barleycorn never had this country boy licked, but I admit he had me on the ropes on several occasions," as well as the hell-raising that went with it. Over a long (81 years) life he saw much of the West, served as a foot soldier in Pancho Villa's army, was a close friend of artist Charles Russell, and in the first days of his writing career avoided volunteering as a subject for an experimental monkey gland operation (the person who did volunteer died as a result of the operation) by selling his first Western to *Argosy* for twenty-five dollars. His second story sold to *Western Story* and he would write continually for *Western Story* from 1923 to 1933. In 1938, he produced a story a month until *Western Story* folded with the September 1949 issue.

He was given the lead story and the cover on every *Western Story* from 1938 through the last issue.

Coburn was the only pulp Western writer to have two magazines carries his name in their titles: *Walt Coburn Western* and *Walk Coburn Action Novels*.

Coburn used a freewheeling, stream of consciousness writing style that was seemingly patterned after his life style: "I liked to have strong setting with the characters based on some cowhand or outlaw, gambler or bartender or lawman that I had known on the range or around some cow town. I turned them loose on paper, let them act out their parts and speak their dialogue. I turned them loose on paper, let them act out their parts and speak their dialogue. I made no notes of any kind but carried the story in my head. I had no plot to start with, so I let the characters do the work, act out the whole yarn, the plot developing as the story unfolded" (from Walk Coburn – *Western Word Wrangler; An Autobiography*).

Coburn died by his own hand at his home in Prescott, Arizona, on May 24, 1971. Walter Brennan, a longtime friend, said of Walt, "I miss him not so much for the things he said, because I can read them in a thousand stories and books he wrote. I miss him for his keen mind and eye as to what was truly Western."

Two of the great Western fiction writers were contributors to the early general fiction and all-Western pulp magazines. Zane Grey had two stories (*Desert Gold* and *The Heritage of the Desert*) specialized in *Popular Magazine* and a few others (*The Light of Western Stars, The Lone Star Ranger, The Desert Crucible, The Border Legion* and *The Roaring U.P. Train*) in *Blue Book* and two Munsey periodicals. Not your average pulp Western writer, Grey would hit it big in hardcover, producing eighty-five books, which sold well over 20 million copies. Besides the pulp Western, especially in the area of the geography and ecology of the West. Grey is also credited with introducing the professional gunman to the Western Story.

Fred Glidden, who wrote under the pen name of Luke Short (in the old West, Luke Short was a gambler-gunfighter contemporary and friend of Wyatt Earp and Bat Masterson), wrote Western pulp fiction for *Western Story, Adventure, Blue Book, Big Book Western, Star Western, Ten-Story Western, Short Stories, Top-Notch, Cowboy Stories, Dynamic Adventures, Dime Adventure Magazine, Ace High, Thrilling Western*, and *Argosy*. Short's Western fiction was firmly rooted in the Western pulp magazines, and he was not embarrassed about his pulp Western pulp background; in fact, the University or Oregon maintains a collection of his pulp Western fiction, and Short attributes his name to the pulp Western editors in a letter to the author mailed shortly before his death:

> The original of the name (Luke Short) is probably well known to you. In the 30s and 40s, pulp editors thought they had exclusive rights to a pen name. Consequently, I had to use a couple of names other than my own. I sent my agent a list of short first and last names. She came up with Luke Short. When I sent my first slick story to *Collier's* and

asked them to use my real name (Frederick Glidden), they declined saying my real name sounded more phony than Luke Short. To this day, I am stuck with it.

Glidden died in the summer of 1974, at which time he was still one of the best-selling authors in print. Short wrote of a West he was familiar with, the American Southwest and Rocky Mountains areas. His work was action-packed in the pulp tradition, and based on first-hand experience of living in the areas about which he wrote.

Brian Garfield has said of Short:

> He had his office in a room upstairs about the post office in Aspen, Colorado, where he divided his time between writing and fishing. It was a room to work in. Nothing more, a reporter's den, a desk, and a window. He was an important citizen in the community, not because of his celebrity status, but because he was, like many of the heroes of his novels, a drifter who had settled down and made himself a part of the community.

H. Bedford-Jones is one of the few other Western writers to rank with Short in the quality of his work (many pulp Western fans hold Bedford-Jones to be the best) and Faust in quantity and style (It has been stated that Bedford-Jones used a battery of electric typewriters to generate three novels concurrently). Bedford-Jones wrote of the heroic West. His stories in *Argosy* and *Blue Book* were epic novels (generally serialized in six parts) of the giants of the early West, Sam Houston, Jim Bowie, Mike Fink, and so forth. The short quotation at the end of the earlier chapter on dime novel Westerns was from a Bedford-Jones story. He was the Homer of the Western pulp magazines.

Wilbur Coleman "W.C.", Tuttle, whose father was a famous Western sheriff, stands out in stark contrast to these other writers. Grey, whose description of a buffalo hunt is textbook perfect; Bedford-Jones, who wrote mainly of the giants of the West, the men who influenced the course of history; and Faust, who wrote the slam bang, slap-leather shoot-'em up action Western. Although Tuttle was almost as popular as the others and his heroes did in fact grace the covers of the same pulp magazines that contained Bedford-Jones and Faust stories, his characters included unlikely comic-relief types:

Henry Harrison Conroy "...was middle-aged, very rotund, and only 5'6" in height. In fact, Henry was so orotund that he had difficulty in crossing his legs, much less putting them up on the railing." and

Rheinlander Strong Pollinger "...was exactly twenty-two years of age, 6'5" tall, and weighted a bare 145 pounds. His face was long and lean and heavily freckled, his hair road, rather than red. His nose was long, his mouth entirely too wide for his narrow face, and he wore horn-rimmed glasses over his blue eyes, which always seemed a bit amazed at the world. Both ears flared a bit, the left a trifle more than the right, as though cocked forward listening."

Tuttle's most successful pulp cowboys were Hashknife Martley and Sleepy Stevens; they prospered for thirty years, starting with an *Adventure* story in 1920;

Hashknife was several inches over six feet in height, with a long serious face, wide mouth, and calculating grey eyes. His raiment was typical of the range country, from battered sombrero to high-heeled boots. At his right, sat a man whose dress was identical to his own; a broad-shouldered cowboy of medium height who wore his sombrero tilted at a rakish angle and gazed with wide blue eyes at nothing in particular; his lips were puckered in an unmusical low-pitched whistle.

Tuttle was one of the few Western pulp writers who could boast of some personal Western life experiences (sheepherder, cowpuncher, forest ranger, and railroader). He was also President of the Pacific Coast Baseball League form 1935 to 1943. Perhaps comedy should be added to Frank Gruber's basic plot list; certainly, Tuttle's thirty-year success with his form in the pulps warrants some consideration.

The Western Writers of America is an organization of writers of Western fact and fiction. Each year, they honor the best piece of Western fiction based on a critical evaluation of all Western fiction produced during a given year. When Ernest Haycox died in 1950, the Western Writers of America called this award the "Ernie," in his honor (it was later renamed the "Spur"). Ernest Haycox is generally ranked as one of the best Western writers, over Faust, Grey, and Short. His first big hit Western was *Stage to Lordsburg*, later made into the movie, *Stagecoach*.

Ron Goulart notes that Haycox did much of his early writing in "an abandoned chicken house with three of its walls plastered with rejection slips." Haycox was influenced by Faust and Grey and prided himself on the authenticity and research behind his stories. He later provided Frank Gruber the necessary reference materials to do Gruber's first (and best) Western, *Peace Marshal*. Haycox wrote for *Western Story* in the early days, but, as his work became more innovative, it also was less acceptable to F.E. Blackwell, who wanted a formula story with no tricks. Haycox wrote additional pulp stories for *Short Stories* and *Frontier*, his complicated plotting and unique style however, led him to the slicks (*Collier's* and *The Saturday Evening Post*), where he got a wider readership and considerably more money, something the chicken coop must have hatched a desire for.

The membership of The Western Writers of America have generally ranked Haycox and Short as the two great practitioners of the art of Western fiction writing. A recent contract of both in *The Roundup* (the official house organ of the WWA) seems to give an edge of Haycox for the quality of his dialogue, his literate style, more carefully drawn characters, and the accuracy of his research. Short's strong points were style (spare and uncluttered), command of dialogue, and ingeniously woven plots. Kent Ladd Steckmesser states in *The Western Hero* that Haycox's *Bugles in the Afternoon* is one of the best historical Westerns ever written, and probably the best novel about the Seventh Cavalry.

Harry Sinclair Drago was a pulp Western regular, and one of the few who worked exclusively in the Western genre. Over the years, Drago did about 25 to 30 stories for *Argosy* and perhaps 100 book-length novels and 50 or 60 short stories for other markets before switching to non-fiction (*The Legend Makers* is one of his recent books). While working in the pulps, Drago spun the epic yarn with enough imagery to give one the sense of being there:

> They were on the Blue the next day. To lose themselves
> in the vastness of the broken, uninhabited plains that
> stretched away to the big bend of the Republican River was
> a simple matter. When they swung westward with it, cross-
> ing into Nebraska, and on the fifth day out found them-

selves on Medicine Creek, fifty miles southeast of North
Platte and the Union Pacific, they had already crossed the
main overland trail from St. Joe. The country that sur-
rounded them now was a wilderness of waving buffalo grass,
threaded by a network of shallow creeks.

Once they had quitted the ridge, they traveled fast,
eyes wary. Prairie hens ran through the grass and refused
to get up until they were almost under the horses' feet.
They sailed away for short distances, clucking angrily at
the intrusion.

Drago wrote for *Blue Ribbon Western, Double Action Western, Argosy,*
Short Stories, and *Western Story Magazine,* using three pen names, Bliss
Lomax, Will Ermine, and Peter Field. This last name was a pseudonym
owned by William Morrow Co., and used by other writers as well. Like
many of the Western pulp writers of the time, Drago spent three years
(1928 to 1932) in Hollywood, working on Tom Mix and Buck Jones
scripts, with a total of 32 motion picture credits. Drago attempted to
start a *Tom Mix* pulp magazine and discussed the project with Mix and
Jack Hill, Mix's manager, at Mix's home. Mix was enthusiastic about the
proposal, wanted to take an active hand in the story preparation, and
promised that, "...they'll all have some truth in them..." Drago later said,
"There was no truth in any of the Mix stories."
Mix did all of his stunt work, but what precisely was Mix and what
was mere legend is delineated in *The Life and Legend of Tom Mix,* by his
cousin, Paul Mix. In any event, the *Tom Mix* pulp never materialized.
Asked to rank the pulp magazines with the best Western fiction,
Drago named *Argosy* first, primarily because of its high overall quality
and equally high circulation (700,000 copies per issue), *Short Stories*
second, and *Western Story* and *Popular* third and fourth. He sold to the
first three only. Harry Sinclair Drago died on October 25, 1979, in
White Plains, New York, at the age of 91.
One of the current best-selling Western authors is Louis L'Amour.
While working in the pulp magazines, L'Amour sold in the neighborhood of 150 to 200 stories of the West to the pulps, in addition to a
number of other short stories. Today, with over 75 Western soft covers
to his credit, he is the most popular (if sales are a barometer of popular-

ity) living Bumppo and "The Virginian." "He was a tall man, wide in the shoulder and lean in waist and hips and easy-moving man with none of the horseman's awkwardness in walking. He moved like a hunter of many things, men not the least among them." More often than not, these are men totally free of family attachments, inclined toward violence as the most handy working solution to the problems presented by the frontier.

In a random sample of ten of L'Amour books, a total of one hundred and fifty-six men die. This figure odes not include those meeting their maker off state (where the non-violent Zane Grey usually committed his mayhem), or in the various general battles, massacres, etc. Violence of not, L'Amour's books has made him the most popular modern Western writer. The pulp Western was his training ground:

> I believe I learned more about writing from the pulps than any other publication or publications. Their demand was for a non-nonsense type of writing, and if one made a living at it there was no time for sitting about twiddling the thumbs.

> I did read the pulps, but none of the pulp writers had any influence on me that I know of, writing for the pulps did have an influence, and that was their requirement that one have a story to tell and that it must move.

L'Amour has tens of millions of copies of his novels in print; more than 30 movies have been made from his books.

Until his death on October 7, 1976 at his home in Norwalk, Connecticut, Tom Curry spent his time between Connecticut and Florida, avoiding the New England winters. Although trained as a chemical engineer, he started writing in college because "it looked like and easy life." With his first successes, he dropped engineering and launched a pulp-writing career that ran into the 1960s, when he was writing both under his own name and as "Romer Zane Grey" for *Zane Grey Western*.

Over the life of his pulp career, Tom Currey produced hundreds of Western novels, innumerable novelettes and short stories, eighty *Texas Ranger* novels, and three dozen *Rio Kid Western* stories. His first Westerns were short and humorous. In 1936, (the 100th anniversary of the found-

ing of the Texas Rangers), he started *Texas Rangers* pulp magazine, and would continue to produce the stories until modern time, alternating with Leslie Scott (under his A. Leslie pen name) and Walker A. Tompkins, all of whom used at various times the Jackson Cole house name.

In a December 11, 1965 *Saturday Review* article, Tom described the apocryphal *Texas Ranger* superhero. "A frontier sheriff in a panic over a range war in his county wires the Texas Rangers for assistance." When he expresses surprise at the single Ranger stepping off the train in answer to his call, the Ranger replies, "There's only one war, ain't there?" This remark has been attributed to "Lone Wolf" Gonzales, whose thirty-one year career with the real Texas Rangers was highlighted by run ins with gangsters, bootleggers, and murderers. Gonzales died on February 13, 1977 at the age of eighty-four.

In 1939, editor Leo Margulies asked Tom to start a new series. Tom played around with a few ideas before hitting upon the concept of a fictional character (the Rio Kid) mixing with non-fictional historical characters and environments. October 1939 saw the first issue of the *Rio Kid* magazine, featuring Bob Pryor, a former Civil War captain, as the Kid, supported by a horse that often appeared smarter than his master. The Rio Kid became quite popular with Western fiction fans, and in 1972, again caught favor with the public in a series of paperback editions reprinted from the pulps. Every other Rio Kid story was written by Tom Curry.

The life of the pulp Western writer was often a curious blend of the commonplace and the exotic. William Colt MacDonald, who wrote all types of pulp fiction, is best remembered for his Westerns and in particular, the here Mesquiteers" characters. Created in *Law of the 45's*, the Three Mesquiteers would ride to glory in the pulps and in "B" Western films. The *Gone with the Wind* of "B" Westerns in *Powdersmoke Range*, a film based on these characters. MacDonald's pulp Western stories were enriched by a pioneering grandfather who had a brief career in pro football, did a little prize fighting, saw some action in World War I, was an amateur painter, refinished Chinese furniture, and worked as a newspaper writer, playwright and poet. MacDonald's Westerns were almost as good as the action in Faust's work, but it was the creation of the Three Mesquiteers that gave him a lasting influence in the Western genre.

One of the most interesting discussions of working during the pulp Western years was provided by Elmer Kelton:

> I came along in the declining years of the pulp magazines. I sold my first story to them in 1947 and the last sometime in the mid-1950s. It is pretty generally agreed that the coming of television doomed the pulp magazines, and though a little slower, all the slick magazines, which specialized in fiction.
>
> I grew up an avid reader of Western stories, both in book form and in the pulps. I lived on a West Texas ranch, near Crane, where my father was a cowboy, then foreman, and eventually manager. The atmosphere was conducive to an interest in this field. A stack of pulp maga-

zines was routine equipment in those days in just about any ranch bunkhouse. Most cowboys love them.

The stories may sometimes have lacked authenticity, and they often exaggerated the action outrageously, but I think the average person in the outdoor. West could find much in them with, which he could identify. They had the flavor of the country he knew, and with this much realism for a base, he could take exaggerations in stride. After all, most tall tales have a base in reality, they usually call for you to accept one far-out premise, but other factors in the story remain rooted to the natural and plausible.

In am sure some pulp writers wrote entirely from imagination and without any real knowledge of the West. But most of the *good* ones were working on solid ground. Walt Coburn, surely the king of the Western pulps, spent his life in the country he wrote about, living among the kinds of people he used in his stories.

Even when the action went a bit overboard, he always kept that aura of reality, that flavor of a real country and real people, acting as they would probably have acted under the set of circumstances Coburn gave them.

S. Omar Barker, the sage of Sapello, New Mexico, was another of my favorite writers when I was growing up on Western pulp stories. Omar's stories, even the serious ones, always had a thread of good humor, and a great many didn't have a serious line in them. He always made his locales real, and the people did what real people might realistically have done, facing whatever situation Omar dreamed up for them.

There were many others. Some like Ernest Haycox, moved on up to a high plane of literature. Others willingly stayed in the pulps for as long as they were active and probably made just as many readers happy.

In my own case, I started out in the pulps with the grandiose intention of using them as a training ground then "moving up to something better." The pulps were hard work and not what you would call extravagant pay. Yet they did pay, and many a good writer served an honorable apprenticeship in them, earning while he learned.

The more I studied the pulps, the greater my appreciation of the better class of stories in them. Until I approached them with an analytical mind and began trying to figure just what made them tick, with of course the intention of using that knowledge for my own benefit. I never truly appreciated the craftsmanship and sometimes outright genius, which were into them.

To a considerable degree, entertainment television today is the modern counterpart to the old-time pulp magazine. It is slicker to be sure, and more money is expended on one TB segment than a pulp magazine might have spent in years. L But the analogy is valid. The plausibility factor is lower in a big percentage of TV fiction than it ever was in the pulp.

The young fiction writer of a generation ago had many outlets for his work. Today, he has few. In an earlier time, he could start at the bottom and work up. Today, he just about has to start at the top, and the competition is fierce. I am glad I started when I did.

Even as a boy, I knew I wanted to write. I used to be poor at athletics and mediocre at arithmetic, but good in reading and English, where only girls were supposed to excel. This led me to a lot of surreptitious writing of fiction stories, which no one but me ever saw. I dreamed up a couple of "great American novels," one of which in concept still seems pretty good to me and I may yet get around to writing it though perhaps in a duskier hue than the rose-tinted version I envisioned at the time.

When I was a senior in high school, and the time came for a decision on how I was to spend the rest of my life, my father asked me my plans. I had abundantly proven that I was never going to be a cowboy; I had two left hands when it came to handling a rope, and even gentle horses put the Indian sign on me. I told him I wanted to go to the University of Texas and study journalism. I wanted to be a writer.

I'll never forget the baleful look he gave me and the long pause before he said, "That's the way with you kids nowadays. You all want to make a living without have to work for it."

But when he decided I was serious, he went along with the idea. I chose the University because I wanted to study under J. Frank Dobie, the Dean of Texas writers. By the time I finished my prerequisites, however, he was gone from the faculty.

After a hitch in the infantry in World War II, I came home solidly determined to get after a writing career. That's when I began taking correspondence courses in addition to a full college load, and dissecting other people's pulp stories like ka biology student whittles at a frog. I began writing stories at a furious pace and mailing them off as frequently as I could afford the postage. I always started at what I thought was the top, Street and Smith's *Western Story* – and often *The Saturday Evening Post*, gradually working down the list as outlined in the *Writer's Market*. The stories always came home unsold.

Then one day, I received a $50 check from Fanny Ellsworth, God bless her, the editor of *Ranch Romances*. She liked a story I had done and thereafter began to take an interest in me. For a long time, she continued to send back most of my stories, but never with the standard, printed rejection slip I had grown to know and hate from S&S and the others.

She always typed up a short letter telling me what was the matter with the story, suggesting changes that might make it salable, or telling me to forget this one but try to remember my mistakes and not repeat them in the future.

Through the seven or eight years that I was active in Western pulp writing, *Ranch Romances* remained my principal market. As the name implies, they used only stories that had romantic subplots, so when I wrote a men-only story it had to go to other pulp markets. Most of these went to one of the Thrilling Publications line of pulps. Occasionally, when I had one that didn't make the grade there at one or one and a quarter cents a word, I sent it to one of the "salvage" markets for a half to one cent a word. I never did get into the higher paying, two to three cent bracket that many more experienced writers regularly drew in the pulps.

The only editor with whom I had any extended correspondence at the time was Fanny Ellsworth. I have never heard from her since she left the magazine in the early 1950s. I don't know if she is still living, but I'll always be grateful to her.

I never had any contact with the artists. The illustrations were always arranged in New York. This is still the case with paperback books. I never have any idea what the cover will look like until I see the finished version. Some Western-story artists were, and still are, very good. Others don't know whether a cow burrows a hole or sleeps in a tree, and their work shows it.

I enjoyed writing for the pulps. I was working full-time as a newspaper reporter, specializing in farm and ranch news for the *San Angelo Standard Times*. My fiction writing was, and still is, a sideline. I am snow associate editor of *West Texas Livestock Weekly*. I remain more a livestock writer than a fiction writer does. I never achieved the production level necessary to make fiction a full-time occupation. Fiction writing still accounts for no more than 20-30 percent of my gross income in most years.

There was a discipline in writing for pulps; a story had to have a good beginning, middle, and a satisfactory ending. By "satisfactory", I mean that things had to work out for the hero; seldom could you get away from a sad ending. Of course, if you wrote a story from the viewpoint of the villain, you always had him get his comeuppance at the end, but that was hardly sad. The story had to have good, steady movement. This did not necessarily mean it had to be permeated by gunsmoke; many of the good pulp stories were long on the *threat* of gunfire but actually had little real shooting.

Characterization had to be strong, but you could seldom get away with the anti-hero types so prevalent today. Your main character in the pulps usually had to be pure in heart and in motive, and steadfast in the face of danger. The James Garner type of reluctant hero would get you a rejection slip, and the Clint Eastwood anti-hero was poison.

Sex rarely crept into a Western pulp. I remember a milk form of shock when in a Wayne D. Overholser story a young lady, not the heroine, showed up with an illegitimate child, and another, also by Wayne, in which the hero and the heroine spent the night together in a barn because of a storm. Nothing untoward happened, of course. *Ranch Romances* was a family magazine. Just being together overnight was far out for the time.

There were always a couple of "spicy" Western magazines on the fringe, but by today's standards, even these were Sunday school stuff. Sex began to creep into Westerns after the paperbacks took over from the pulps. It has never taken a very stronghold, even yet. The average Western today approaches sex obliquely, if at all.

I leave the spicier material to the younger writers, who approach the subject more comfortably than I ever could. I have the traditional inhibitions of my generation. Too, there is always the problem of basic research.

This reminds me that Zane Grey usually had a sexy scene in most of his Westerns of the 1920s and 1930s...sexy by the standards of the time, at least. Usually, at some point, the heroine was in dire peril of the proverbial fate worse than death. It never happened, of course. At the late Stephen Payne once said, "The pulp heroine was 'often chased', but ever chaste."

I never was a heavy producer and I probably sold less than 100 pulp stories, ranging from 5,000 word shorts to 20,000 word novelettes. As pulp writers go, I was never any factor in the market. Though after the first couple of years I managed to sell virtually everything I wrote, I was still essentially a novice to the end of the pulp era.

After 30 years as a writer, I still feel like a novice. About the time, I think I have things figured out; they change the rules on me. I read books and see movies today, which have no beginning, no middle, and no end. They seem to drift along on a stream of consciousness, and when the last page comes or "The End" flashes on the screen, I am still waiting for the point.

Life is never as pat as it seemed in the pulp stories, but neither is it as pointless or directionless as it seems in some of today's fiction and films.

I have no particularly original ideas on the reasons so many people like the Western. In its traditional form, it is usually a fairly straightforward action-adventure story with characters who are interesting but not complex enough to cause the reader undue strain. The story moves at an agreeable pace, providing a quota of vicarious armchair thrill that add up to relaxation and entertainment more than to education or enlightened.

Some writers, and I include myself, try often to build a story around authentic history and give the reader some insight into a real time, place, or situation. We often try to put across a theme or a viewpoint, perhaps paralleling a historical situation with a present-day situation or problem. We attempt to do it subtly, however, and try never to beat the reader over the head with it, for we realize his main interest is entertainment. If he wanted straight history, he would have gone to a non-fiction work rather than to a short story or a novel. We try to give him history and reality as a bonus.

I find that the Western writer today has considerably more freedom than he had a generation ago. If he chooses, he can be more realistic in many areas, including sex, racial relations, and character motivations. It used to be almost mandatory to pull all the loose ends of a story together at the finish and tie them up in a neat bowknot. But real life had a lot more slip-knots than bow-knots. I have found in recent years that I can do a story in which all the problems aren't solved, in which the lead character can face the same unresolved frustrations as we everyday mortals. In short, the ending of a Western story today needs to be logical, but it does not have to be totally happy or have all its problems resolved.

Even the relaxation reader today has been conditioned to expect realism he would not have accepted in the pulp days, or which, at least, the pulp editors were unwilling to try on him.

There are today as many types of Western stories as there are Western writers. There are probably more, because few writers do all their own stories alike. If your taste runs that way, you can still find the traditional "head-'em-off-at-the-pass" actioners in which fast movement and simplistic characters dominate. You can find heavy histories and psy-

chological Westerns more skin to Tolstoy than to Zane
Grey. Or, you can find the modern blend, which uses
some of both worlds, going for more realism, but never
turning its back on the basic elements, which have kept
the Western alive and well since Ned Buntline dreamed
up his first big lie about Buffalo Bill.

True West ran an excellent article in its February 1967 issue ("Twenty-
Five Years of Glory for the Western Pulps"), which featured some personal
reminiscences of an old Western pulp fictioneers, J. Edward Leithead.
Leithead wrote for many of the leading Western pulp magazines, and,
having been an Indian buff from his early reading of Cooper's Leather
stocking Tales, was constantly trying to introduce Indians and related
themes into his fiction but with little acceptance from the editors. Some
pulps, however, did run "nonfiction" columns; for example, *Real Western
Stories* used "The Red Man's Story," a series of "true fact" articles by one
White Eagle (Sioux); these were supposedly intended to examine the role
of the Indian in American history. *Real Western's* "Mail Pouch" column
often received mail sympathetic to the Indian, for example: "It's high time
that the public should learn that there has been an immense amount of
anti-Indian "propaganda" pushed down our throats, that the Indians were
patriots defending their homes and freedom, that the whites were almost
always the aggressors, and that many of the atrocities attributed to the
Indians were actually committed by the white man."

White Eagle may well have been Max Schwartz of the Bronx, but this
was pretty mature and timely stuff when you contract Parkman's observations: "The Ogillallah, the Brule, and the other Western bands contact
with civilization." Leithead had some success in introducing Indian subjects but on the whole, Western pulp fiction ignored the Indian's cause,
Of Gruber's seven basic story types, only the "Custer's Last Stand" category specifically requires the presence of the Indian, and then only in a
highly unfavorable light insofar as most white Americans are concerned.
L Again, perhaps the Gruber categories should have been expanded to
include a story type that featured the Indian and his view of the West and
the Western expansion movement of the white man.

The name Hal G. Evarts is familiar to most readers of pulp Western fiction, as two generations of writers worked the pulps with this name; Hal G.
Evarts, Sr. sold his first story to the long-vanished *Top Notch Magazine* in

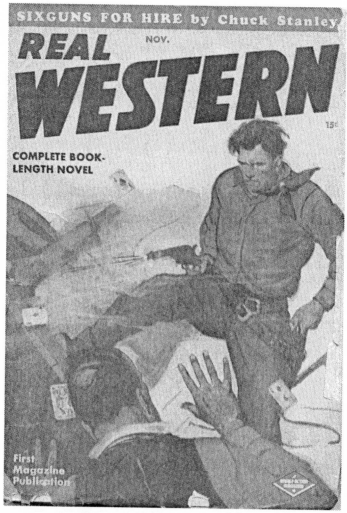

1919 for $150, and "never did another honest day's work after that." Hal G. Evarts, Jr. worked in *Adventure, Argosy, Thrilling Western, Ranch Romances,* and *Zane Grey Western* from 1941 to 1953, but did most of his Western writing in the 1950s and 1960s. Evarts, Jr. casts his vote for *Adventure* as the pulp with the best Western fiction. Today, Evarts is writing novels for young readers (Charles Scribner's Sons); as a former member of Western Writers of America, he has met and known dozens of ex-pulp Western fictioneers, but sadly reports their ranks are thinning fast. He ranks Faust as the best pulp Western writer, and cites Ken White (*Adventure*) as one of the great editors.

Wayne D. Overholser worked from 1936 to the end of the pulp era in the 1950s, and is phenomenally successful today as a writer of West-

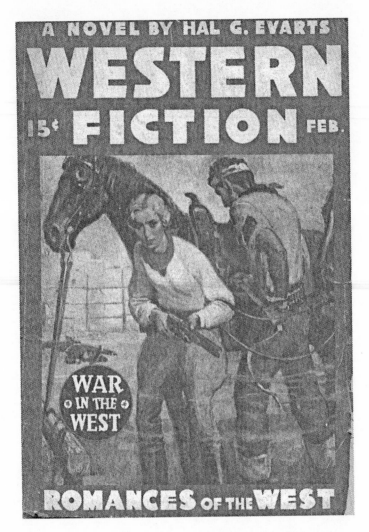

ern novels (as in his son, Steve), largely for Dell and Ballantine. Overholser wrote about 400 stories under his own name and under the pseudonym Emmet J. Powell, mainly for *Ranch Romances*, the Popular string, and the Standard magazines. His choice for the best in Western pulps are *Dime Western*, *Ten-Story Western*, and *Ranch Romances*; and he rates Walt Coburn as the most popular Western pulp fictioneers, and Harry Olmstead and Tom Blackburn as the best. Other ex-Western pulp writers he maintains contact with are Ray Gaulden, Doc Collins, and Willis T. "Tod" Ballard.

Overholser was one of a few pulp writers, Western or otherwise, to be receiving hardcover reviews in the *Saturday Review* in the early 1950s. He later collaborated with Spur-winner, Lewis B. Patten, on several paperbacks, proof indeed that the paperback Western was as much a vehicle of survival for the Western pulp writer as it was an instrument of death for the pulp era. Patten, who has done all types of Westerns from *Gene Autry and the Apache War Drums* to his Spur-winning *Red Sabbath*, is one of the few Western writers to have had his words translated into German and Spanish. When asked about his strongest or fondest memories of the old Western pulp fiction days; Patten replies: "Regular checks coming ten days to two weeks after submission." Patten's manuscripts, books, and correspondence are being maintained by the Western History Research Center of the University of Wyoming.

William MacLeod Raine was one of a handful of foreign-born pulp Western pros. Born in London in 1871, Raine came to the United States, settled in Colorado in the early 1900s, and began to write. He wrote for the early golden pulps such as *Argosy*, and for the dime novels. Raine had one of his stories in the first issue of the first Western pulp magazines, *Western Story*. Raine used the rancher-sheepman type story (Gruber's number two plot), with a dash of mild sex, and it had an authentic ring to it. Over the years, Raine wrote a few hardcover Westerns, and in the early 1950s, he was the Dean of the Western pulp writers. Raine explains the attraction of the Western:

> The West was not only a geographical area. It was a
> hope, a state of mind, a dream, a utopia… It was neigh-
> borliness, fear, and courage… It was the fine free feeling
> of an outdoor life in the saddle. It was the strong sense in
> each man that he was an individual that he was on his
> own. And it was because of all these things and so much
> more that its glory must be kept alive in an America that
> is prone to forget its proud past.

Raine died in 1953, and has since been elected to the National Cowboy Hall of Fame (one of only three writers so honored); he was made the first honorary president of the Western Writers of America.

B.M. (Bertha Muzzy) Bower (nee Bertha Sinclair, the Bower came from the first of three husbands) was on of only a few women writers to make her mark in the field of Western pulp fiction, and she would make the transition to hardcover Western fiction as well. Her first novel, *Chip of the Flying U*, was originally published by *Western Story* and later re-printed in cloth. It was the only material of Bower's to be made into a movie (Universal, 1947, with Johnny Mack Brown). Born and raised in the frontier West of the ate 1880s, she began writing in the first quarter of the 20ᵗʰ century, and produced two novel-length Westerns yearly until her death in Los Angeles in 1940. Her stories were entertaining Westerns much along the lines of the *Bonanza* television series, and her character-izations were significantly better than those of the fun-of-the-mill pulps. Republished by Popular Library in the 1940s and later reprinted in the 1950s and the 1970s, her original editions are sought-after collectors' items today. Bower's Westerns were realistic yarns of the frontier West spiced with some romance in the grand tradition of *The Virginian*. They often reflected a bias against farmers, who were generally the villains in conflict with the ranchers. As noted by collector Roy Meyer, "Not only does she know the life of the cowboy, but she knows the country in which he lived." Bower talks about her background and qualifications in the fol-lowing autobiographical letter published in the December 10, 1924 issue of *Adventure*.

Much to my regret, I was not born on the range, though my parents, pioneering in the "Big Woods" of Minnesota at the time, did kindly provide me with a log cabin to be born in. They gave me Sioux outbreaks for bedtime stories and some real pioneer blood in my veins, and for these I am grateful. That blood came drop by drop from that melodramatic man, Miles Standish, who did carry his gun over his shoulder to church and per-formed many other movie stunts that must incur the dis-pleasure of certain convention-loving critics. It runs in the blood, for later on a certain Colonel Robert So and so (bearing the name) fought with Washington and liked it so well that home life palled. He left his family and went exploring in "the wilds of western New York State," and lived among Pendexter's Indians "of the Long House," I have no doubt. I never can remember whether he left six children for eight years or eight children for six years. Long after he was believed to be very dead and scalped, he calmly returned.

It does surely run in the blood, for my father kept edging into the West. When Minnesota was admitted as a State and Sioux gentled down, life turned stale, evidently, for he took us into Montana when Great Falls was "Jim" Hill's new boomtown and wild as you want them, and a boxcar was called the depot, I remember. From that time on, I lived among cattle and cowpunchers, so perhaps I do know a little about it. My father taught me music and how to draw plans of houses (he was an architect among other things) and to read *Paradise Lost* and Dante and H. Rider Haggard and the Bible and the Constitution, my taste has been extremely catholic ever since then. From *Paradise Lost to She* in one evening was quite a jump for a kid, but he encouraged me to make it.

This by the way of showing was the pioneers of the Northwest were like, a good many of them. For the life of me, I can't remember that they were sordid and forlorn, and I never knew any gaunt, hungry, etc., pioneers up Montana way. I have traveled a good bit throughout the West, from Juarez to Lethbridge, from St. Paul to Seattle, and points in between and down and around and back and forth. I've visited pioneer towns and men as Mr. Henry no doubt has haunted art galleries and old cathedrals in Europe. I wish to go on record as saying that, as far as my personal knowledge of them goes, and all I have read and heard, the real pioneers of the range are well worth knowing for themselves. They are and have been alert, given to thinking things out for themselves, quick to see the dramatic element in their lives, why, if one old-timer has urged me to write his life "because it sure would make the greatest book you ever read," a hundred of them have offered themselves.

What became of the "gaunt, homely, hungry" men and women of Mr. Henry's West? Those men who, with "their few women-folk furnished figures too weazened, weary, forlorn for the buoyant pages of adolescent pageantry?" Many and many I knew, and they cherished the memory of their hardships, their fights with Indians and storms, and the wilderness. As for the women, listen to this chronicle of fact.

Very soon after the time of Hough's story, not more than five years later, James Alexander Cowan, called Jim, started north with a trail herd of two thousand head of V7 cattle from Texas, near Fort Worth, and took h is wife and two children with him, and household gods and goods. They wintered in Ogallalla, then started on in the spring and trailed up into Colorado, just under the Wyoming line. There they settled and raised their family. Mrs. Cowan, far from being weazened and weary, taught her children music and kept a regular school during the winters so that her boys left her tuition only to enter the University of Wyoming.

When the Indians under Colorou burned the cabins and the piano that had been freighted in with terrific labor, she took a board, marked on it the keyboard, and went right on teaching her children music. They grew up excellent musicians, all of them, I believe. She used to stand in the doorway and shoot antelope that trailed past the cabin. She fed and "mothered" the Indians when they were at peace, and then they were "up" they would send word beforehand than an outbreak was due, whereupon the Cowans would retire to Fort Sanders, where Laramie now stands, and stay until the uprising had subsided, then go back and build up their ranch again. IN my *Cowcountry*, I had described that trail herd and family, in a general way.

A year or so following the settlement in Colorado, a herd of V7 cattle was driven to the Canadian line by Cowan's partner, one Barney Hunter. Montana was stocked with Texas cattle driven north on the Chisholm Trail and its extensions. Balch & Bacon drove up the Block-dulap herds. The Circle Bar came into Northern Montana from Texas and so did the old NL herd. I doubt if there was ever so small a herd as one thousand cattle driven north, because for so long a trip men would scarcely think it worth while; like one man driving alone in a big seven-passenger car, just as easy to drive with more passengers. Two thousand head was considered a nice, easy number for eight riders to handle. I have the world of the boy who went north with the V7's, and who later on drove up other herds, that forty-five hundred head could be handled easily enough by ten riders. From two to three thousand, however, made up the ordinary herds that went north. Until the railroads offered a quicker transportation, trail herds went up to and even into Canada, in the Sweet Grass and Cypress Hills ranges. There are plenty of old-timers who are still alive and able to tell all about it.

Later the herds for Montana were shipped to Billings, and I have described that phase of the work in my *Lure of the Dim Trails*. I was asked to write about cattle and took the Montana range for my subject, using the shipping of Texas cattle to Billings, and the drive north from there, as an incident of the story. This was in 1905, and the story was laid in 1886 or thereabout. But until Billings became a shipping point the herds were trailed up to the northern ranges.

I do not think the Cowan family was an exception to the general run of pioneers. When you stop to think of it, the kind of men and woman Stuart Henry imagines the range pioneers to have been could never have met the test, which life gave daily to the cattlemen. They had to be made of good stuff. They had to think for themselves, and think quickly. A weary, weazened, hopeless and forlorn type could not have existed under the conditions they would have to meet. That would be a psychological impossibility.

As a matter of fact, the forlorn and hopeless ones never had the imagination and the initiative to leave home and strike out boldly into the wilderness. The first pioneers who came west must have had an ideal, which they followed. I am not speaking now of morals nor guessing how many men who had gone wrong, fled into the West to escape the law; but even so, they had imagination and courage or they would never have attempted it.

Certain mental qualities were an absolute necessity to survive the hardships and the dangers. Courage, patience, a quick, sure judgment, that imagination, which we now call "vision," and a big, sympathetic spirit of helpfulness were all a part of the mental equipment that could meet emergencies and turn unexpected developments to advantage. These qualities never can and never will develop a sodden, hopeless, slow-thinking breed of men and women devoid of imagination and the sentiment that makes for romance. There are certain fundamental laws of metaphysics, which can not be ignored, and there is no getting away from the fact that "As a man thinketh in his heart, so is he." The men and women who had to depend on their wit and their endurance and their initiative for their existence *could* not be clods.

Those very qualities did, however, produce the six-gun type. From meeting and interpreting emergencies according to their own individual judgment, men came to making their own laws and enforcing them. They developed a hair-trigger pride that magnified their own importance and made mountain insults out of molehill offenses. That, I take it, was initiative and imagination run amuck. I venture to say that there never lived a six-gun bad man who hadn't a warped kind of pride in himself and what he called his honor; a childish passion for impressing his individuality upon those around him. They *had* to respect him and fear him and jump when he spoke or take the consequences. I've heard "bad" men boast, and that was the burden of their thoughts, a determination to be hailed master among their fellows. It's an ideal as old as humanity itself.

The women, you must remember, were the mothers, the wives, and the sisters of the men. There were hundreds of them, and I never met one of the colorless, forlorn types. All the pioneer women I never knew were past middle age, by the time I was old enough to take notice, and they were alert, vibrant with interest in all that went on around them, ready to talk your head off, usually, and never happier than when they could talk and talk of past adventures and paint in all the dramatic highlights. If they were weazened and forlorn, hopeless, drab things in their youth, in heaven's name what happened to perk them up so amazingly in their old age? You see, by all the laws of psychology, of metaphysics really, it simply won't work out that way.

I knew one sweet, soft-voiced little woman who moved into Idaho with her three children just a few days after the "Mountain Meadow massacre." She used to talk by the hour of her experiences during Indian outbreaks and gold rushes, and times when she took her children to the stockades during the uprisings, and cooked for the men and nursed the wounded and said prayers over the dead.

She painted in the romance of it and the thrill, the love and the laughter and the tragic scenes. She was a young widow living with her father and brother, and wooers were many, I judged. A movie serial could be kept going for months on the stories she told me. And there were hundreds of such women throughout the West. They and their men-folk were a type distinct, fascinating to one who loves to delve into fresh made history. I can tell an old-time Westerner at sight, and never yet failed to make overtures toward friendly acquaintances, not with the curiosity of the tenderfoot goggling after "types," but because I have tested the breed and found it always worth knowing. Rough, unlettered, perhaps, though not always that. But the lack of what we are pleased to call culture was always filled with a personality that went deep into hearts that had known how to ache and how to leap for joy, how to walk boldly with death, how to make merry with the simple pleasures and the simple emotions of life.

Yet I appreciate Stuart Henry's protest against overemphasizing the whoop-er-up, six-gun side of the West, and I can add my voice to the protest. Violent death is not all you see in the eyes of the pioneers. There's more of loneliness and monotony in pioneering than there is of battle. I can personally vouch for the fact that pioneering was, and still is, about ninety percent monotonous isolation to ten percent thrill. It is scarcely fair to turn the picture upside down and present the public with ninety percent thrill and ten percent normal, everyday living. Days and days pass slowly by and then, *bing!*, something breaks loose and you are living raw, drama. Ask any old-timer who learned to put on his hat before he pulled on his breeches, and to turn his books upside down and shake them to make sure a rattler hadn't crawled in during the night. Wild times do come to those who travel the dim trails. I speak in the present tense deliberately. They do not seem to breed weazeness and solidness nowadays, at any rate.

The "buoyant pages of adolescent pageantry" have not all been turned, take my work for it, because I am living through a few chapters right now.

Bower's pulp stories were published in *Argosy, Popular Short Stories, Adventure, West Magazine,* and *Western Story Magazine.* These were her early works. All of her later stories (17 novels) were hardbound.

Erle Stanley Gardner ran his own ranch; worked with cowpunchers of the 90,000 acre Vail Ranch on long roundup drives, spent time in various Western locales such as Rhyolite and Randsburg, and otherwise, qualified himself with firsthand Western experiences in order to write good Western fiction for the pulp magazines. In spite of this background and his considerable writing skills, he found the going tough in the Western pulps. On more than one occasion, he had a story rejected for lack of authenticity by a "knowledgeable" pulp editor. For example, an editor once maintained that a particular story would have been acceptable if it hadn't had so many assayers located in the mining town of Randsburg, supposedly the miners really didn't need assayers. Gardner sent copies of plans of the real Randsburg's main street, showing an "Assayer" sign over every other door.

Gardner's Rhyolite story concerns a cowpoke who falls in love with the daughter of a wealthy snobbish Eastern woman who can't see her daughter throwing herself away on a mere cowpoke. The cowboy quits his job, takes up residence in Rhyolite (population three, the cowpoke and two bodies), has himself elected mayor, invites the mother and daughter to town (as mayor), and marries the girl while the future mother-in-law is incarcerated for some minor legal transgression by the "sheriff" (one of his buddies). As it turns out, Rhyolite was a real Western town, and the legal circumstances described in Gardner's tale were, in fact, something of a legend. Upon reading the story, however, the editor informed Gardner that he had let his imagination run wild in creating Rhyolite, and that his readers simply would not accept such far-fetched story. It came as a shock to Gardner that the esteemed editor of a Western pulp magazine didn't know of Rhyolite, so he sat down and informed the editor in a "very nice letter" that not only did the town exist, but that the legal points in the story were based on fact, after which came a long stream of rejection slips.

Al Gibney, head editor of the Munsey pulps, had his picture taken by Gardner while outfitted as a cowboy and posturing as he was about to clip a cow's ear. All of this took place at Gibney's request when he and Gardner were guests on the Vail Ranch. Gibney actually fainted when he tried to cut out a section of the cow's ear, but the picture as described by Gardner showed Gibney bossing operations, and Gibney had it framed and hung over his desk in his New York office. Months later, Gibney sent a letter to Gardner telling how he had had a visit from one of his more prominent Western writers, who had clacked down the hall in his cowboy boots, slapped his ten-gallon hat against his legs, and offered Gibney a big "Hi-yah pahdner," while placing the boots on Gibney's desk. Spotting the picture, he said, "My God, Al, it's you!" to which Gibney responded, "Sure, I was ramrodding the Vail spread for a while, did you know that?" "Good God, no!" the man said. Gibney went on to say that the visit was short and sweet, and when the writer left the office, he must have tiptoed all the way to the elevator, because Gibney, listening carefully, couldn't hear the sound made by the boots' high heels. After a few such experiences with the Western pulps, Gardner threw in the towel, saying he could no longer see anything dramatic about the life of a cowboy. He was more successful with Perry Mason.

Elmore Leonard is one of the more successful ex-pulp Western fictioneers, having had much of his recent work made into movies, including *Mr. Majestyk, Joe Kidd, Valdez is Coming, Hombre, The Big*

Bounce, 3:10 to Yuma and *The Tall T.*; the last two were from original pulp stories published in *Dime Western* and *Argosy*. Elmore's first sales was a big one (*Apache Agent* to *Argosy*), netting $1,000 in August of 1951; and he went on from there to do about thirty short stories and five novels (all Westerns) for *Argosy, The Saturday Evening Post, Blue Book, Zane Grey Western Magazine, Dime Western*, and a few others. All of this was done on a part-time basis while cranking out advertising copy for Chevrolet, and writing educational films for *Encyclopedia Britannica*. The sale of his oft-rejected *Hombre* to the movies in 1967, five years after its publication, gave Leonard the freedom to pursue writing as a full-time occupation. Paul Newman starred in the film, which probably helped make it so popular.

Looking back on the pulps, Elmore has mixed feelings, "I can't say I really missed the pulps when they passed away, because I wasn't relying on them then for a living. But I'm sure glad they were there at the time." One the other hand, a note from Fred Manfred (a Western writer who "tried to write them like they'd last forever"), puts pulpish nostalgia in a slightly different light:

> I used to read Western pulps in the local Doon, Iowa, drugstore, I couldn't afford to buy them so on Saturday nights, I'd stand reading them at the newsstand until I was chased away. When I went out shock thrashing in the summer, I always made it a point to visit the neighbor's privy in the hope that someone might have nailed up a Western pulp for wipes. When I found one, I took a real crap!

Gordon D. Shirreffs is another successful Western pulp writer who has made the transition to paperbacks. Gordon's start in Western pulps fiction stems from his reading and enjoyment of Zane Grey, Ernest Haycox, and Clarence Mulford in the pulps, and his interest in military history in general and the Civil War in particular.

> One of my early favorites was *Battles and Leaders of the Civil War*, which I first started to read about 1926, at the age of 12. Later, in 1940, I was stationed at Ft. Bliss, Texas, with an anti-aircraft artillery regiment called up from the Illinois National Guard and attached to the First Cav-

alry Division. While there, I spent my free time in the deserts and mountains hunting for lost mines, sites of long-abandoned forts and posts, battle sites, etc., and became intensely interested not only in the army in the West, but also in the Confederate invasion of New Mexico, which of course I had known about for fifteen years. As far as my knowing the West, I think I can qualify, as in the past thirty-five years I have covered most of it, hunted, fished, looked for lost mines, lost treasures, etc. My favorite shooting rifle is a black powder Sharps Old Reliable buffalo gun in .50/.90 caliber. No man can call himself a rifleman until he has put twenty rounds through that cannon. I knew and talked with old-timers of West Texas, who had ridden with Billy the Kid, others, all gone now. Knew an army sergeant who had served at Wounded Knee as a recruit. I should have recorded these conversations.

Between 1952 and 1955, Shirreffs sold about 150 Western stories (army-oriented) to Popular, Standard, and other publishing houses. Since those days, he has written for the paperbacks and cloth publishing, many of his stories featuring a man-hunting theme, as embodied in his character, Lee Kershaw. Many have been published by Fawcett Gold Medal Books, and some, like *Rio Bravo*, have attained near-classic status.

A large number of writers "minored" in the Western; that is to say, they were primarily science fiction or detective fiction writers, but sold to the Western pulps when taken by the need for a quick sale or when the demands of quantity pulp writing compelled. Hugh B. Cave, for example, wrote mostly horror and detective fiction among his 1000-plus pulp stories, perhaps 50 were Westerns. Cave's Westerns appeared in *Nickel Western, Western Story*, and *Two-Gun Western*, all under his own name. Unfortunately, Cave lost the majority of his original manuscripts in a fire and as a result of moves made over the years from Haiti to Jamaica to Florida, where he now lives. Today, he is doing books (war, travel, and horror) and exclusive magazine material for *Good Housekeeping*. A collection of his horror fiction was published late in 1977 by Carcosa House under the title *Muirgunstrumm*.

L.P. Holmes worked the Western pulps from 1925 to the bitter end of the pulp era under various pen names (Matt Stuart, Dave Hardin, and Perry Westwood), as he says, "You name a Western pulp and I was in it at

one time or another." He has nothing but gratitude of the career provided him by the pulps:

> A swell, rewarding life. Was my own boss. Lived much of my life in the kind of country I wrote about. Knew a lot of characters who fit into my yarns perfectly. Writing for the pulps was fun, a never-ending adventure. Good days. Bad days, but always interesting. Glad I was part of the pulp era. As the old saying goes, "All of it I saw, part of it I was."

Bill Cox also speaks well of the pulp days:

> I dwelt mainly in Florida, made a fine living, had all the
> time off I wanted, played tennis every day. All my associations
> with editors and publishers were good, bar none. I was in *Blue
> Book* as Joel Reeve for fourteen years, the best of relationships.

Cox wrote Westerns starting in 1940 when as he puts it, he'd oversold
the other markets, mainly sport shorts, and, as in his yearly wordage output
approached 600,000, he went looking for new subjects. His Westerns were
as popular as his sport stories, most were in the W.C. Tuttle vein. His
principle Western character was Duke Bagley, a sort of Whistler Kid. More
recently, when "Jonas Ward" died (his real name was William Ard), Cox
took over the "Buchanan" series in paperback for Fawcett Gold Medal.

Willis Todhunder "Tod" Ballard was primarily detective fictioneers:

> For myself, I sold my first pulp story to a magazine called
> *Brief Stories* in 1928, for which I received $75 for a ten-thou-
> sand-word novelette. I was not writing full-time in those
> days. I began in 1930 when the Depression had ruined my
> job. I sold my first Lennox story to *Black Mask* in 1931, and
> continued selling that magazine until well after Capt. Shaw
> left. In those days, I wrote six Lennox novelettes, three Red
> Drakek stories, and two Don Tomasso stories every year. In
> all, I managed to sell Shaw three more stories each year than
> Erle Stanley Gardner, a fact for which Erle never quite for-
> gave me. For ten years, until the start of WWII, I averaged
> better than 100,000 words a year. Most of this was detective
> copy although I did do a few Westerns for the better class
> magazines, mostly *Short Stories* and *Blue Book*.
>
> After I returned to the coast from Wright Field in 1946,
> the pulps were already on their way out. You could not
> give a detective away in Hollywood so I switched to the
> Western books, which I could sell to *Esquire* for serial
> rights. MacMillian and Houghton Mifflin for cloth books,
> Popular Library for paperback reprints, and Republic and

Columbia for pictures. Also, I tried to turn out five or six books a year, with the result that I now have one hundred and eleven, which with sales to foreign countries, have averaged better than one half million copies each. I have also done over fifty screen and TV scripts. [*Ballard died at age 74 in Mt. Dora, Florida, on December 27, 1980*].

The old pulp writers tend to refer constantly with pride to word output and sales production. No one in the business looked down his nose at quantity and for good reason. Quantity was one of the primary contributions made by the pulps to the reading public, as well as being utterly necessary to any pulp writer who wanted to make a decent living by writing. Even the better-known writers produced enormous quantities of fiction, most under multitudinous pseudonyms.

Frederick C. Davis, a name well known to fanciers of pulp literature, worked mainly in the detective pulps (at the rate of one story per week), but did manage also to sell a few Westerns, including a "Duke Buckland" series for *Western Trails* in the middle 1930s. Buckland (alias Jack Spade) traveled about avoiding the law with a boy side-kick, Kit McCane. Although Duke usually got involved with one or more girls in each escapade, each story ended on the same note (Freud and Wertham take notice): "Far across the hills, Duke Buckland and Kit McCane were riding the owl-hoot side by side, the trail that would never end."

Roland Krebs started writing the no-gun W.C. Tuttle-type Western for *Western Stories* in the early 1930s, featuring shorty Nolan of the R Bar R, a ranch peopled by the likes of Hungry Hosford. The offbeat adventures of the R Bar R bunch generally took place in The Last Hitch, one of Sufferin' Cat's two saloons. Sufferin' Cat had been given its name by a drunken faro dealer. This kind of Western provided well-needed comic relief form the steady diet of shoot-'em-ups, but they were merely a diversion.

The one man who has lived through the three pulp Western periods, and who, more than anyone else, embodies all the positive qualities that went into the pulp Western, is S. Omar Barker. Mentioned frequently by his peers as the writer they most admire, elevated by unanimous vote of the Western Writers of America to Honorary President (only the fourth so honored, the others being William McLeod Raine, Charles H. Snow, and Dwight D. Eisenhower, a self-confessed Faust addict), Barker has been recognized officially by the WWA "for bringing honor and dignity to the Western legend." Squire Omar Barker ("Lazy S.O.B," was his brand when he had cattle), had a sixty-year writing career, as well as stints as a rancher, politician, poet, solider, and teacher. His honors include a pair of Spur awards, and an honorary chieftainship of the Kiowa Tribe. He had the good fortune to marry a lady (Eva McCormick) who was nearly his equal with the pen, and who was frequently published in *Ranch Romances* over the years. Not to be overshadowed by his spouse, Omar sold short stories and a "Know Your West" column, which ran in each of 250 consecutive *Ranch Romances* under the pen name *"Rattlesnake Robert."*

Over his writing career, Barker published about 1500 short stories and novelettes, 1200 fact articles, and some 200 poems. Although his experience in ranch work was limited to his father's farm, he wrote mainly what he knew, stories of the ranch and range country, of old-time cowboys and the old West, nothing more recent than the 1920s in setting. Some of Barker's poems are about such simple subjects as the meaning of the various sounds made by cattle. His best-known work is a poem, "A Cowboy's Christmas Prayer," which has been recorded by Jimmy Dean and Tennessee Ernie Ford, and broadcast on national networks in America and England. Omar's writing almost always has the cowboy's sense of humor, in a recent issue of *The Roundup*, he rambled on with obvious delight how *Strange Tales* bought a yarn of his after it had been previously rejected seventy-five times, and then proceeded to fold.

Over a period of several years, I've managed to communicate with many of the people who worked in the pulps. Of this group, some wrote in many genres, while others took a quick turn at the Western only to discover that one's ignorance of subject matter was more transparent here than in the detective, sports, or other yarns. Of the writers who specialized in the Western, many (like a number of us in this age of rapidly changing technology) learned how to do what they were doing while they were doing it. A few managed to combine the necessary writing skills with a sense of humor and a set of roots somewhere West of Yonkers to produce both entertainment and sometimes enlightenment for the more than one million people each week who bought and read the Western fiction magazines.

"Gone are the old-time stars that inspired the adulation of millions. Youngsters of today tend to worship different idols. But the Western picture as entertainment or as an art form, in a world beset by violence, uncertainty, and fear, will probably continue to provide an escape for millions of Western fans for years to come."

– Joseph G. Rosa, *The Gunfighter, Man or Myth*

To "B" Or Not To "B"— The Pulps & the Movies

Pulp writers played a significant role in providing grist for the Hollywood mill. Many of the silent and talkie Westerns were right off the pages of the pulp magazines, and more than a handful of pulp fictioneers would serve a rewarding term or two working and reworking Western scripts.

If indeed the Western story is one of the few Native American art forms, and the motion picture the artistic medium of the twentieth century, the writers of Western pulp fiction have little or no credit for the creation and translation onto film of the Western theme. The pedigree of the Western film actually parallels the evolution of the Western theme from its early dime novel days through the pulp era to the paperback Western of today.

Dime novel readers were thrilled with the film exploits of Bronco Bill Anderson (actually Max Aronsen of the Bronx) in 1903, when *The Great Train Robbery* was playing nickelodeons across the country. It didn't really matter that Max couldn't stay on a horse long enough to complete a scene; Western films, the good and the bad, would prove to be a permanent staple of the American entertainment diet.

Over the years, the Western film had its peaks and valleys, 30% of all films produced in the 1926-27 season were Westerns, while the percentage was down to 1% in the 1929-30 period. From this point through the 1950s, there was a gradual increase in the public appetite for the film

123

Western; this peaked in the 1958-60 period, when one-third of all feature films made in those years were Westerns, with thirty-seven weekly Western series on TV. During the 1960s, the Western virtually disappeared from television, and managed to hold on in the theater due mainly to the success of the foreign-made "spaghetti" Western.

The silent films used up considerable dime novel material making hundreds of fifteen-act serials *a la Pearl White* and *The Perils of Pauline.* A press release of the day (1921) boosts male lead Joe Ryan:

CRACK SHOT, RIDER IN WESTERN FILM:

> If there is a single man who can typify the best there is in the West of prairie and mountain, that man is Joe Ryan. Ryan now spends most of his time acting for the screen.

> But Ryan isn't a film "Westerner." Ryan merely does the things he has always done, the things he could do expertly since he could walk, and a camera man makes a record of them, which explains why thousands of fans the country over rejoiced when it announced that he would appear in *The Purple Riders*, a splendid virile Vitagraph serial, with a Western setting and a stirring, unusual plot.

When the fifteenth "act" of a serial was shown, some enterprising theater owners of the day would also show the first "act" of their next serial, thus adapting the narrative "hook" to their own financial gain. With the exception of some of William S. Hart's films (and Hart was one of the greatest hambones of all time), the silent Western film was a potboiler whose success was based on two ingredients; the new-found toy aspect of film entertainment, and the personal popularity of its virile stars, Frank Farnum, Buzz Barton, Jack Hoxie, Art Acord, Tom Mix, and others.

By the time the talkies had replaced the silent flicks, Hollywood producers were looking for historical characters such as Buffalo Bill, Billy the Kid, or Jesse James, or fictional heroes like the Cisco Kid. Warner Baxter's *Cisco Kid* was the first of a long string to feature a fictional hero, and marks the first use of sound recording techniques out-of-doors. Johnston McCulley's Zorro was another Western pulp superhero with lasting power on film. Douglas Fairbanks, Sr., first brought the fictional avenger of

America's southwest to the screen in the 1920 release, *The Mark of Zorro*. The first talking Zorro film was in 1936 with Rober Livingston (later to play *The Lone Ranger*) in the role. The star of the first Zorro serial, *Zorro Rides Again*, was John Carroll. Famed stuntman Yakima Cannutt did most of the Zorro acrobatics, with mask in place, except for the film with Douglas Fairbanks, whose agility and poise in the role would never again be matched. The 1939 Zorro flick starred Reed Hadley, while the forties saw George Turner and Clayton Moore (also to play *The Lone Ranger*) in the familiar black costume. Ken Curtis (*Gunsmoke's* Festus) and Richard Simmons (TV's *Sgt. Preston*) played Zorro in the 1950s before Walk Disney bought the character rights and cast Guy Williams in the role. Frank Langella and Alain Delon did television versions in 1974 and 1975. The big "Z" has also appeared in the "spaghetti" Westerns. Other than Zorro, the great gifts to the Western film from the pulps were the Hopalong Cassidy films and the Three Mesquiteer films.

Clarence E. Mulford wrote for the silent Tom Mix films in the 1920s and later would have his "novels" rewritten and filmed for the Hopalong Cassidy series. These sixty-six films, produced by Harry Sherman, were the most successful "B" Westerns ever made, with the possible exception of the Gene Autry musical Westerns (many of which were written around a theme song, which doubled as the film title). The initial six Cassidy Westerns (*Hopalong Cassidy, The Eagle's Brood, Heart of the West, Three on a Trail, Call of the Prairie* and *The Bar 20 Rides Again*) were all based on the original pulp character, a scruffy, working cowboy. The remaining sixty films were potboilers, with Bill Boyd in the saddle as a cleaned-up, somewhat older version of the pulp "Hoppy."

William Colt MacDonald was the pulp writer bidding the Tree Mesquiteer films, which include, *Powdersmoke Range* in 1935 (this film had in its cast just about every "B" Western film cowboy Republic Studios could get its hands on, Harry Carry, Hoot Gibson, Bob Steele, Guinn Williams, Buzz Barton, Wally Wales, Buffalo Bill, Jr., Franklyn Farnum, and others), and *Law of the .45's* in 1935-36. In addition to *Powdersmoke Range* and the other Three Mesquiteer films, which grew out of MacDonald's original Three Mesquiteer pulp yarn, *Law of the .45's*, MacDonald's film credits include *Range Feud* (1931), with Tim McCoy, *Two-Fisted Law* (1932) with Tim McCoy, and the six Mesquiteer films done in 1938 and 1939, *Santa Fe Stampede, Red River Range, The Night Riders, Three Texas Steers, Wyoming Outlaw*, and *New Frontier*, which featured the team of John Wayne, Ray Corrigan, and Max Terhune. Many other "B" Western stars, including Robert Livingston, Duncan Renaldo, and Al St. John, would play in these films, all of which featured much action and gunsmoke.

Certainly, the biggest impact by the pulps on the film Western was due to the presence of Frederick Faust in Hollywood. Prior to setting up shop permanently in the film capitol in 1938 at $1,500 per week, where he would amaze his peers by turning out fifty pages of script material a day (the norm was between 10 and 15), Faust had seen many of his pulp Westerns turned into movies including, *The Best Bad Man, The Flying Horseman, Destry Rides Again, Dark Rosaleen, The Cavalier*, and so forth. Actors who appeared in Faust Westerns included Francis X. Bushman, John Gilbert, Douglas Fairbanks, Sr., Tom Mix, Humphrey Bogart, Marlene Dietrich, Jimmy Steward, Joel McCrea, Barbara Stanwyck, Lew Ayres, Lionel Barrymore, Lorraine Day, Rita Hayworth, Alan Ladd, Audey Murphy, and many more.

Alan LeMay was one of the many pulp writers to spend a few years in Hollywood in the 1920s and 1930s, doing Westerns. His two most popular Western stories are *The Searchers* and *The Unforgiven* (1956 and 1960). Other Western pulp writers and their films were, Frank Gruber (*The Kansas, Broken Lance, Quantrill's Raiders*), Ernest Haycox (*Stagecoach, Union Pacific, Bugles in the Afternoon, Trail Town, Canyon Passage*), Luke Short (*Blood on the Moon, Ramrod, Station West, Vengeance Valley, Coroner Creek, Silver Rock, Ride the Man Down*), Harry Sinclair Drago (Tom Mix and Buck Jones flicks), Gordon D. Shirreffs (*Rio Bravo*), Elmore Leonard (*Hombres*), and C.S. Boyles (*Man of the West*).

Television kept the "B" Western alive for another decade after its cinematic decline in the early 1950s, with *Hopalong Cassidy, The Cisco Kid*, and *The Lone Ranger*, whose goals seemed to be to put the heroes back in the saddle again.

The year 1955 would bring about a maturation of the Western and kill off the "B" Western forever, with the initial showing of the so-called "adult" Western, and action Western with greater dramatic rendition. These included *Wyatt Earp, The Rifleman*, and *Gunsmoke*. *Wyatt Earp* and *The Rifleman* are refined heroes, or as the popular culturists would say, knight's errant. In any event, these two TV Westerns were in the tradition of *The Lone Ranger* and *Hoppy*, while *Gunsmoke* told the classic frontier. Luke Short type of Western (Sheriff Version), where the conflict of the frontier was centered right there in the The Longbranch Saloon. The soap opera or "Empire" Western (*Bonanza*) was a descendent of the Haycox Western, and surfaced in 1959, running here and abroad through the 1970s.

In the peak TV Western, years of 1956-60, there were as many as 37 Western series at one time on the tube. By the time, the Western pulp magazine was long gone, with the sole exception of a few digest-sized Westerns and a pulp-type magazine that was published into the 1970s by Popular Library, *Treasury of Great Western Stories*. This "treasury" was all reprint material. There were no new Westerns being written in the old pulp format.

"They used to say that Pop Hines would crop off the head of Whistler's Mother if he thought it would fit the page better"

— Howard Muncie describing Pop Hines, head of the Street and Smith stable of artists, from Quentin Reynolds *Fiction Factory*

Beneath a Pastel Sun—
The Artists

"I think I have learned and pictured just about every fancy way of disposing of human life known to man"
— L.R. Gustafson in "Who's Who in *Blue Book*," October, 1938

"There is a slight flaw in the cover painting, but perhaps the reader won't notice that Jim Dawson wears a mustache in the picture though he is described as clean-shaven in the text"
— Harold Hersey in *Pulpwood Editor*

In the 1930s and 1940s, the Western pulp was basic escapism. The world was a pretty dreary placed at the time, suffering from economic woes and preparing itself for a second World War in one generation; the pulp Western was a way out of this trap for a few hours (for two bits of less!). The splendid newsstand array of pulp Western cover art was an experience in lust that saturated the senses with visions of gunsmoke and rearing horses, gunmen being shot down, damsels on horseback in distress, clutched by villains firing six-shooters with their free hands, poker tables being knocked over, leather being slapped. Pulp cover art was the come-on, the lure to bedazzle.

Once the purchase was made, a private place had to be secured for communion with this magazine, a department, or two at a time, then settling in for one's first story choice. Once into the text, the cover art would be periodically referred to in order to refresh one's imagery; some-times-difficult if the prose didn't quite match the luscious cover art. Such flaws often occurred, because most cover art was commissioned independently of the fiction, and few editors cared to take the time to match the cover art with the feature story. In any event, pulp art was the art of the masses (as paperback art is today), and based on the proliferation of these magazines, it was certainly a vital part of the Western pulp experience.

While largely a subjective matter, many fans and critics regard H.W. Scott, R.G. Harris, Walter Baumhofer, Norm Saunders, and Nick Eggenhofer as the premier Western pulp artists. *Life Magazine* ran a two-page spread on Scott (June 29, 1942), in which they called him the world's most prolific illustrator (his average was something less than two covers per week), noting that Scott had planned to be a pianist until he had suffered a compound fracture in World War I. Baumhofer's output equaled Scott's (at least in 1935, when he produced a total of 84 paintings), and his work for the Street and Smith chain had a rugged vitality that seemed to embody the individualism and toughness of the frontier cowboy. His feel for the Old West made him on of the most popular of all the Western pulp cover artists. Baumhofer always painted his Western covers in oils, his first being perhaps his most memorable:

> "I suppose a high spot was the contract Street and Smith gave me to do 50 covers a year in 1933, which effectively ended our part in the Great Depression. We (my wife is an artist too) had been down to our last $100 but instead of paying the rent, I spent $30 on a model, at $1.00 per hour (the going rate at that time), on a quite-detailed speculative Western cover and they were crazy about it. I got more and more covers to do for them, including *Doc Savage* and then the 50-cover contract."

Baumhofer studied on a scholarship at Pratt Institute and attributes his style to influences by the Spanish painter Sorolla, and such American illustrators as Howard Pyle, N.C. Wyeth, Pruett Carter, and Dean Cornwell. Like many of the pulp cover artists, Baumhofer did not know which stories his paintings would illustrate:

> "At Popular, Harry Steeger, the publisher, Ellsworth Terrill, the editor, and I would hash out an idea between

us, and the poor author would have to fit the incident into his story, even though some of the ideas were pretty wild."

Nick Eggenhofer's pulp cover work came a long way from the early days, when he began illustrating Westerns as newly arrived immigrant who had never been west of the Hudson River. His work can now be found in expensive coffee-table editions such as Northland Press' *Fifty Great Western Illustrators*, and on the masthead of *The Roundup*, the Western Writers of America house organ.

Raphael DeSoto worked in more pulps than he cares to remember, including *Dime Western, Ace Western, Red Seal Western, Star Western*, and *Western Story*, all in addition to his work in the non-Westerns, *Adventure, Detective Tales, The Spider, Black Mask*, and many others. DeSoto was one of the best, if not the best, detective cover artist and he enjoyed doing the Western covers as well. "They had to have action, color, six-shooters spitting fire, hero in trouble, but no defeated, and no girl kissing!" DeSoto's pulp work is quite collectible today; some of it was recently exhibited at the State University of New York Farmingdale, Long Island.

Edmund J. DeLavy lives and paints in a studio home, which he designed and built on the west bank of the Rio Grande River near Bernalillo. A native New Englander form Kittery, Maine, DeLavy came west to visit and explore in 1947, when he was doing pulp Western covers for *Ranch Romances* and *Giant Western*. As a young student just out of school, DeLavy's most pleasant memories of the pulp days centered on his trips to Street and Smith, and while sitting in the waiting room, marveling at the vast panorama of *Shadow, Doc Savage, Western Story*, covers on display there. DeLavy's subject is still the West and his paintings of working cowboys and other Western subject matter are in collections all over North America.

Shorty Shope painted covers for *Lariat* and *Triple-X* as well as doing book illustrations and commission work. His work was influenced by famed Western artist, Will James, whose views on the value of a university education were penned to Shorty – "Schools are all right but the most important things are learned out of them places" and by Charles Russell, who told Shorty, "Stay with the West boy, the men, the horses, and the country you like and want to study are here." Shorty heeded Russell's advice and went on to fame and success in the Western art field, his work being exhibited and sold at the Grand Central and Kennedy Art Galleries in New York and at the Desert Southwest Gallery in California.

James L.L. Mendlik, president of Western Galleries, Inc., provided me with background material on R. Farrington Elwell (1874-1962), a first-class Western illustrator whose work includes interior pen and ink illustrations, covers, hardcover, and slick work, and oils and pastels on canvas. Elwell has been favorably compared with Catlin, Remington, and Russell. Elwell both wrote for and illustrated the early pulps such as *Everybody's*, and was one of the few artists or writers who brought authenticity to the pulps.

R. Farrington Elwell was also Buffalo Bill Cody's best friend and lived with Cody on his ranch in Wyoming from 1897 to 1917. While Elwell was with Cody, both Russell and Remington visited the ranch to hunt and fish with Elwell. Elwell had traveled from Boston with the Cody show as a youth in order to pain Indians, cowboys, and the West, and became known as the "Russell of Arizona." The current price range for original Elwell oils is $10,000 to $15,000.

A few other great American artists to work in the early pulps are N.C. Wyeth (*The Popular Magazine*) and Herbert Morton Stoops (*Blue Book*), both of whom did cover work. Stoops also did some interior work under a pseudonym.

Over the three pulp Western periods, a number of artists would do some very exciting action covers for the Western pulps, Larry Bjorklund, Gerry Delano, Joe Lyendecker, Bill Kremer, Fred Craft, Rudolph Belarski, and my personal favorite Western cover artist, R.G. Harris, whose style encompasses painstaking realism, perhaps his best cover was on the August 15, 1936 issue of *Wild West Weekly*.

While some of the Western pulp artists were born to the trade, others like Graves Gladney were as eclectic as their brother writers:

> "I began to do Western pulp covers because they were 'open', i.e., the covers for the Westerns were produced by those who worked on speculation. Fiction House was a small publishing company with three or four titles, among them, *Lariat*. Coached by Emery Clarke, Tom Lovell, and John Falter, I produced a painting with two galloping horses on which a cowboy and his lady were escaping for dear life. I shudder now each time I see a reproduction of that cover, like most Westerns, it was phony as a three-

dollar bill. I painted it for acceptance on a rainy day in 1937. I had .25 in my pocket and my heart in my mouth. After an agonizing period of silent inspection, the two editors said, "We'll buy it; make out a check for $75." So I was now a paid painter as opposed to the art-for-art's-sake fine artist.

Next, I performed the same miracle on *Rangeland Romances* and *Star Western* of Popular Publications, both owned by ace bad man, Harry Steeger. There were others, best forgotten, but my best Western was oddly enough done for *Adventure*, and depicted a cowboy departing sadly on foot after destroying his injured horse. Steeger bought that one too, much to my surprise and paid handsomely (for those times). Among the various painters in New Rochelle, New York, there were props for any Western picture, chaps, boots, spurs, etc. I borrowed some of these and could beg, borrow, or steel anything lacking a model (anyone from printers' apprentices to elevator operators would do). The chosen one donned the uniform, struck the pose, and we were off and running. Mostly, we took photographs of the action and worked from these, supplying the horses from any source, photos in magazines, newspapers, or whatever. As soon as I began to sell my pictures regularly, and with a guarantee of acceptance, I dropped Westerns like a hot coal.

The remainder of Gladney's pulp cover career was spent working in the detective genre for *Shadow* magazine, and for some horror pulps. Gladney died at his home in Clayton, Missouri, during the summer of 1976.

As with the writers, the pulp artists constituted the last cottage industry that targeted the casual "mom and pop" store customer in an effort to entice him with lurid action color covers and eventually part said buyer from his ten cents. They did the job well enough and as a group, can take considerable credit for the fantastic number of those magazines that sold over the counter every week.

"Manley shot again, into the dust, moving a leg to support him. Then the gun fell. He tried to say something and could not. He raised a hand to his chest and his left knee buckled. He fell, kneeling, and then pitched gently into the dust"
                              – Luke Short's classic description of a gunman's demise

The End To the Trail—
The Demise of the Pulp Fiction

"For an endless moment, he teetered back and forth like a gnarled oak – stricken unto death but unwilling even now to be brought to earth. He crumpled up at last and sank to the floor with a tired sigh"
                              – Harry Sinclair Drago's version

"To the explosion, the Kid uttered a scream, whirled around and the gun was jerked from his hand and flung across the one room of the shack. He fell sideways, and lay there groaning and cursing"
                              – H. Bedford-Jones

The pulp Western caught one between the eyes in 1953-1955 but like Short's expiring gunman, managed to stumble and stagger into the 1960s before finally dropping into the dust. The flashily-covered, ragged-edged Western pulp is no more. For a combination of reasons, including rancid prose, hoof-and-mouth disease, paper shortages, television, competition from the commercial slicks, and a conspiracy among the distributing companies to kill the pulps generally in favor of more lucrative fare, the horse opera, as embodied in principle and charm by *Big Book Western*, was the first to go, and was survived only briefly by the soap horse opera,

Ranch Romances, Romantic Range, etc. Famed Street and Smith editor Daisy Bacon attributes the demise to yet another source:

> "These people, managers, took the magazines off course into alien and uncharted waters and in the process; they killed the goose that laid the golden egg. It was said of one magazine house that they spent most of their time in making out schedules for press releases. They felt they were running a news service instead of publishing magazines."

With their demise, the preservation of the old Western pulp yarn has become the major concern of fans, collectors, and historians. We have seen in recent years a film, *Hearts of the West,* based on a young man who, enthralled with the contents of *Big Book Western,* sets out to attend a non-existent Western Writing University to master the knack of producing pulp prose, only to wind up a short-lived "star" in a "B" Western film. The fiction itself still lives on in Western paperback reprints, prominent names in the Western fiction section of any current bookstore include Raine, Brand, Evans, Overholser, Short, the same names, and stories, featured in the pulps of thirty or forty years ago. Many of these men, Faust/ Brand for example, were so prolific that "original" books still appear under his name every year. The source material for their many reprints, the original manuscripts and pulp magazines, are still sought out and preserved by private collectors. In addition to the collectors' efforts to preserve the magazines, there has been some organized effort to collect and catalog them. Public repositories include the UCLA Library's Special Collections area, 18,000 pulps of all genres, the Library of Congress' "substantial collection," the University of Wyoming's and the University of Oregon's special collections of several Western pulp authors' correspondences, manuscripts, teleplay scripts, and original pulp magazines.

Also, at least in certain quarters of the world, the pulp still lives. Ben Haas was good enough to send a couple of European Westerns, whose format is nearly identical to American pulps of forty years ago, glossy, action-packed, slick-covered magazines with pulp-like interior pages, the same old purple prose, and even similar advertising. I wrote to Finn Arnesen, editor of *Western,* and asked him about the reasons for the popularity of Western story in Europe:

Western has been published continuously from the autumn of 1956, initially fortnightly, then for a good many years as a weekly magazine. From 1974, we changed the format to double what it had been and in size, the magazine is now like *True West*. We publish mainly fiction, plus a few factual articles. The magazine is now published every fortnight again, and we sell approximately 25,000 copies of each issue.

Why is the Western story popular in Europe? I believe that most European readers read Westerns purely as adventure stories, not having any knowledge about the history of the West and the background for the stories. There is, however, an increasing number of younger readers who are really interested in historical facts, and who want more authentic and realistic stories. The old "Wild West" makes for very colorful and dramatic reading, and provides an arena where a lone man can administer justice with the help of hard fists and a gun. I think there is a longing in people living in very well regulated, modern societies for the primitive and uncomplicated life of the Old West. Nowadays, a criminal may commit an unlawful act, a quite brutal one, and society must wait for a year or more before some sort of justice is dealt out. In the old days, a lawman just went out and gunned the killer down in a duel. It was uncomplicated and fast, and at least gives the illusion of a freedom that people long for. I think there is a lot of romantic nostalgia in it, but of course, the main reason for the popularity of the Western is that the stories are exciting, action-packed, and provide relaxing reading.

In most other European countries, the popularity of the Western has had its ups and downs. In Norway, the Western has always been popular. During the last 25 years, publishing Western pocketbooks has been a lucrative business and you can always be sure of a good sale. It is a fact that throughout history, Norwegians have been adventurers, the Viking employers. Perhaps there is a certain national spirit more prominent in Norwegians than in other Europeans that makes us long for excitement. This is purely a theory; the fact is seen in the non-stop popularity of Westerns in Norway. My magazine, *Western*, is as far as I know, the only European publication of its kind. Similar magazines have tried in Sweden, Denmark, and other European countries and they have all folded. There are some True Western magazines, especially in Germany, but *Western* is the only magazine in the old pulp magazine tradition.

In Norway, the most popular type of Western fiction is the modern, realistic story with a factual background, also with a bit of sex and a touch of brutality. The old romantic style (I always think of it as the Zane Grey epoch) has had its day. I still print some short stories form the 1930 to 1950 American pulp magazines in *Western*, but that is mainly because so few stories are written by American Western writers today. People don't believe in the hero gunning down a gang of bandits and then happily riding away into the sunset, strumming his guitar. They don't believe in a heroine blushing furiously when her long skirt slides up and her ankle is seen.

They want a hero who may throw up after he has killed a man, who is changed and brutalized by his own acts of violence. They want women of flesh and blood, with sexual cravings. They want realism.

Stories of this kind are without the slightest doubt the most popular ones. In Norway, the stories written by the Norwegian writer Kjell Hallibing, pen name Louis Masterson, by far outsell all other Westerns and all other fiction. We print 80,000 copies of each new novel he writes; the norm for most Norwegian pocketbooks is 8,000 to 12,000 copies. Hallibing is, by the way, a very good writer who has been hailed by the serious literacy critics of our biggest newspapers as one of the best Norwegian writers in the last 25 years, who has been compared favorably with Jack London.

We also publish Ben Haas' novels about "Fargo", which are not number two in popularity in Norway. His stories are also rough, realistic, with a bit of sex and a factual background. We print 30,000 copies of his books and sell most of them.

We also publish novels and stories by English Western writers. The earlier works of J.T. Edson were popular. Unfortunately, he is now writing very complicated novels with a lot of foot notes and is trying to put in so many facts and so much information that his stories are frankly unreadable, in my opinion. Readers are not looking for encyclopedias; they want excitement first.

Peter Watts is another British writer. Under his pen name Matt Chisholm, he is writing very good novels and short stories, with quite a bit of humor. That is another element that makes for popularity. The humorous story is always popular. Watts also knows his West and his stories are exciting adventures. We print 18,000 copies of his novels. He is also writing short stories for *Western* magazine, as is another British writer, Mike Linaker, under then name of Neil Hunter.

I am buying short stories for the magazine from American writers like Thomas Thompson, Bill Gulick, D.B. Newton, Wayne C. Lee, Lewis B. Patten, Elmer Kelton, and others, whom I have met at the conventions of Western Writers of America. Other popular American writers in Norway, and in Europe, are Louis L'Amour, Luke Short, Max Brand, and most of the other well-known ones.

As a rule, I think you may say that European Westerns tend to be more brutal, describing violence in more detail and having a stronger element of sex than the stories written by Americans. Some writers go much too far, like the Englishman writing the "Edge" series, and write speculative stories, basking in blood, abnormality, and sex. I don't believe in this kind of story, more than I believe in the so-called "spaghetti" Western movies. They may be popular for a while but then the public loses interest, the same as for pornographic movies and stories. In the long run, the public wants tough, hard, fast-moving stories but without too may gory details and over-done sex scenes. They want a factual background and like stories where the fictional hero is moving among authentic figures like Billy the Kid, Wild Bill Hickok, and so on, or where the fictional hero takes part in historic events like the battle at Little Big Horn, or the showdown at OK Corral.

There are a number of young Norwegian writers who are attempting to write these kinds of stories for *Western*, and I try to direct their writing to fit into my own belief of what the public wants.

Unfortunately, most of the American Western writers are getting old and very few of the young writers try their hands at Westerns. The older writers are a bit too traditional. They know how a Western story ought to be told and are not willing to change their way of writing to fit our modern, more liberated tastes. By this I don't mean to say that for instance, the earlier novels of Lewis B. Patten or the moving short stories of Thomas Thompson will ever be old-fashioned or out of style. I just mean that America needs a new generation of writers treating the Western story in a modern way, like perhaps Ben Haas.

I doubt if the old pulp Western format will return in America. *Black Mask* and *Weird Tales* took a shot at reviving the format and were very quickly pulled off the newsstands. The pulp spirit may be alive abroad, even there it is arrested developmentally somewhere in the late 1930's, artistically languishing between *Western Story* and *Wild West Weekly*. Those who have the old spirit are not interested in the new breed of Western writers of the hardcover or paperback formats. They want the original musty-smelling magazines and they want to recreate the old thrills when all one's senses were assaulted by the pulps' vitality.

Sturgeon's Law, that 90 percent of anything is crap, applies as much to the pulp Western as it does to other genres. Most of the fiction in the Western pulp magazines was junk prose dealt up to non-critical audiences by indifferent editors and hack writers. Usually, everyone in the chain from writer to editor to reader was largely ignorant of the real West. A handful of Western pulp writers could, on good days, produce an occasionally memorable story. The Western pulp story was mass entertainment for an unsophisticated audience and on that basis, it worked very well indeed. Read by millions of adolescents, the working classes, and the poor, the pulp Western provided a combination that was welcome in the 1930's – escape from a depressed and depressing world, and cheap, instantly-gratifying entertainment. The pulps offered an instant morality play that gave hope and comfort to the masses by offering escape to the secure fictional world of an Old West that never existed. The pulp Western writers as a group were a fascinatingly heterogeneous bunch. The idea of someone from the Bronx cranking out "original" Western material created low comedy both on and off the pages of the pulp magazines. Finally, the pulp Western was an art form of sorts. While the concept of the frontier is not exclusively America, the details of frontier conflicts and their resolution within the framework of the horse opera is a peculiarly unique ritualistic drama that reaffirms the American experience. America's spirit has always been at the frontier as it moved westward. On a good day, the Western pulp wordsmith captured all of that and more and gave us all a lot of fun in the process. For me personally, musty odors and all, the Western pulps still ring the bell.

"The past went that-a-way. When faced with a totally new situation, we tend always to attach ourselves to the objects, to the flavor of the most recent past. We look at the present through a rear-view mirror. We march backwards into the future."

– Marshall McLuhan

Afterword

The passing of the Western pulps was a powerful passing as a style of living passed along with it—the cowboy life. We were all city kids but we lead the cowboy life. It started with the Tom Mix radio show in 1933 and continued on through childhood. None of us had ever seen a cow but we knew the cowboy through the daily radio dramas of Tom Mix and the goings on at his Bar Z Ranch. The stories captured the ears, hearts and minds of my gang and we couldn't wait to act out the then universal play of 'cowboys and indians,' which was enhanced by the great premiums one could get by simply mailing a dime and a Ralston boxtop to Checkerboard Square, St. Louis, Missouri.

We chased each other firing imaginary six-guns or lossing one arrow after another from dawn to dusk. The kids who got to play the cowboys were those whose parents could afford a piece or two of a kid cowboy outfit at the downtown dime store; the kid version of the ten-gallon hat would do. At the end of the day we returned to the radio to hear yet another Tom Mix adventure, all the while aware of Tom's Straight Shooter Pledge:

I pledge to shot straight with my parents by obeying my father and mother.

I promise to shoot straight with my friends by telling the truth always, by being fair and square at work and play, by trying always to win, but being a good loser if I lose…

And so forth.

And those gorgeous Tom Mix premiums allowing us to share in Tom's real time adventures, "for a Ralston box top and a thin dime" you were transported into Tom's radio dramas.

When we outgrew the kid game of cowboys and indians we graduated to cowboy cards. There were a number of these but my favorite was the set produced by Hassan Corktip Cigarettes. Needless to say we were dependent on either finding an adult in our life who smoked this brand or ceaselessly searched the streets for discarded cards. This series of cards pictured daily events in the cowboy's life. They were collected, traded and scaled to a wall (closest takes all cards) and stored away at home with the same feelings Silas Marner had for his gold cache.

In my early teens I noticed this six-gun blazing in my direction. It was held by a mean-looking cowboy and he was riding right at me. The cowboy of the pulp magazine was the kind of cowboy we saw in the B westerns every Saturday—a hard riding, slap-leather western hero; a man's man. If you had just a dime to spend it was a tossup between a cowboy pulp and a B western movie featuring the likes of Bob Steele, Buck Jones, or Lash Larue. Each, in its time, fulfilled the need.

There were rodeos at Boston Garden and you heard Der Bingle singing "Don't Fence Me In" and the Sons of the Pioneers singing of Dan's travails in "Cool Water" and then there was that day you first saw the copy for the Red Ryder "Golden-Banded Daisy":

> "Picture yourself riding the range with the husky RED RYDER CARBINE lashed to your saddle thru the authentic Carbine Ring...loading her up with 1000 shot in just 20 seconds...drawing a bead through the adjustable DOUBLE-NOTCH REAR SIGHT. Then...Bang... Bang...Bang!...as fast as you can work the CARBINE COCKING LEVER...up to 1000 shots without once reloading!"

No kid who led the cowboy life could resist this pitch which set us on a mission to a) convince Mom you wouldn't put your eye out and b) raise the $2.95 price. For most of us it was a dream unfulfilled but a minor loess in view of what was coming.

Sometime in the 1950s all of this went away...kids no longer had a cowboy life...the radio shows, rodeos, premiums, pulps, games of cowboys and indians, cowboy 'pitches'…nothing was left but the sweet memories, not even the cowboy songs. Pundits argued the causes but their answers would not change the fact that the cowboy life had gone the way of the running board, and this was the larger loss.

Bibliography

The information used in preparing *Pulp Western* was obtained directly from the people who wrote, illustrated, edited, published, read, and/or collected the various pulp western magazines. The principal information sources were the western pulp magazines themselves.

Background information was obtained from a number of secondary sources. The major sources and other related sources are listed here for those who wish to expand the scope of their reading of the roots of nineteenth and twentieth century popular western fiction.

Of these, the two which best complement *Pulp Western* are, *The Dime Novel Western*, which surveys popular western literature in the era preceding the pulp magazines, and *Comics of the American West*, which covers the same subject in the post-pulp magazine decades.

Austin, James C., and Donald A. Koch, eds. *Popular Literature in America.* Bowling Green, OH: Bowling Green Univ., Popular Press, 1972.

Barbour, Alan G. *The Thrill of it all.* New York: Macmillan, 1971.

Blacker, Irwin R., ed. *The Old West in Fact.* New York: Ivan Obolensky, 1961, ed. *The Old West in Fiction,* New York: Ivan Obolensky, 1961.

Branch, E. Douglas. *The Cowboy and his Interpreters.* New York: D. Appleton, 1927.

Braver, Ralph, and Donna Braver. *The Horse, The Gun, and The Piece of Property.* Bowling Green, OH: Bowling Green Univ. Popular Press, 1975.

Browne, Ray B., Marshall Fishwick, and Michael T. Marsden, eds. *Heroes of Popular Culture*. Bowling Green, OH: Bowling Green State Univ., 1972.

Browne, Ray B. "The Popular Western." In *Journal of Popular Culture*, Vol. VII, No. 3. Bowling Green, OH: Bowling Green State Univ., 1974.

Carroll, John M. *Eggenhofer: The Pulp Years*. Fort Collins, CO: Old Army Press, 1975.

Caswelti, John B. *The Six-Gun Mystique*. Bowling Green, OH: Bowling Green Univ. Popular Press, 1971.

Daniels, Les. *Comix: A History of Comic Books in America*. New York: Bonanza Books, 1971.

Dobie, J. Frank. *Prefaces*. Boston: Little, Brown, 1975.

Dorson, Richard M. *America in Legend: Folklore from the Colonial Period to the Present*. New York: Pantheon Books, 1973.

Durham, Philip, and Everett L. Jones, eds. *The Frontier in American Literature*. New York: Odyssey Press, 1969.

Easton, Robers. *Max Brand: The Big Westerner*. Norman, OK: Univ. of Oklahoma Press, 1970.

Engen, Orrin A. *Writer of the Plains*. Culver City, CA: Pontine Press, 1973.

Etulian, Richard W., and Michael T. Marsden, eds. *The Popular Western*. Bowling Green, OH: Bowling Green Univ. Popular Press, 1974.

Farley, G.M. *Tom Curry: A Half Century of Westerns*. Williamsport, MD: Zane Grey Collector, 1975.

Fenin, George, and William Everson. *The Western*. New York: Grossman, 1973.

Frantz, Joe B., and Julian Ernest Choate, Jr. *The American Cowboy: The Myth and the Reality*. Norman, OK: Univ. of Oklahoma Press, 1955.

Fussell, Edwin. *Frontier: American Literature and the American West*. Princeton: Princeton Univ. Press, 1965.

Goodstone, Tony. *The Pulps: Fifty Years of American Pop Culture*. New York: Bonanza Books, 1970.

Goulart, Ron. *Cheap Thrills: An Informal History of the Pulp Magazines*. New York: Arlington House, 1972.

Gruber, Frank. *The Pulp Jungle*. Los Angeles: Sherburne Press, 1967.

Harmon, Jim, and Donald F. Glut. *The Great Movie Serials: Their Sound and Fury*. Garden City, NY: Doubleday, 1972.

Hersey, Harold. *Pulpwood Editor*. New York: Frederick Stokes, 1938.

Higham, Charles, and Joel Greenberg. *Hollywood in the Forties*. New York: A.S. Barnes, 1968.

Horn, Maurice. *Comics of the American West*. South Hackensack, NJ: Stoeger, 1977.

Horwitz, James. *They Went Thataway*. New York: E.P. Dutton, 1976.

Jones, Daryl. *The Dime Novel*. Bowling Green, OH: Bowling Green Univ. Popular Press, 1978.

Keiser, Albert. *The Indian in American Literature*. New York: Oxford Univ. Press, 1933.

Lahue, Kalton C. *Bound and Gagged: The Story of the Silent Serials*. New York: Castle Books, 1968. *Winners of the West: The Sagebrush Heroes of the Silent Screen*. New York: A.S. Barnes, 1970.

Lupoff, Dick, and Don Thompson, eds. *All in Color for a Dime*. New York: Arlington House, 1970.

McCarthy, Todd, and Charles Flynn, eds. *Kings of the B's: Working Within the Hollywood System*. New York: E.P. Dutton, 1975.

Miller, Don. *Hollywood Corral*. New York: Popular Library, 1976.

Mix, Paul E. *The Life and Legend of Tom Mix*. New York: A.S. Barnes, 1972.

Monaghan, Jay. *The Great Rascal: The Life and Adventures of Ned Buntline*. New York: Bonanza Books, 1951.

Mott, Frank Luther, and Theodore Peterson. *Magazines in the Twentieth Century*. Chicago: Univ. of Illinois Press, 1956.

Noel, Mary. *Villains Galore: The Heyday of the Popular Story Weekly*. New York: Macmillan, 1954.

Parkinson, Michael, and Clyde Jeavons. *A Pictorial History of Westerns*. Norwich, England: Jarrold and Sons, 1972.

Pearson, Edmund. *Dime Novels: or, Following an Old Trail in Popular Literature*. Boston: Little, Brown, 1970.

Reitberger, Reinhold, and Reinhold Fuchs. *Comics: Anatomy of a Mass Medium*. Boston: Little, Brown, 1970.

Reynolds, Quentin. *Fiction Factory: or, From Pulp Row to Quality Street*. New York: Random House, 1955.

Rosa, Joseph G. *The Gunfighter: Man or Myth*. Norman, OK: Univ. of Oklahoma Press, 1975.

Savage, William. *Cowboy Life: Reconstructing an American Myth*. Norman, OK: Univ. of Oklahoma Press, 1975.

Smith, Henry Nash. *The Virgin Land: The American West as Symbol and Myth*. Cambridge: Harvard Univ. Press, 1950.

Steckmesser, Kent Ladd. *The Western Hero in History and Legend*. Norman, OK: Univ. of Oklahoma Press, 1965.

Wector, Dixon. *The Hero in America*. Ann Arbor: Univ. of Michigan Press, 1963.

White, David Manning, and Robert H. Abel, eds. *The Funnies: An American Idiom*. New York: Free Press, 1963.

Williams, James Robert. *Cowboys Out Our Way*. New York: Scribners, 1946.

Index

Ace High Magazines, 52

Arensen, Finn, 136

Bacon, Daisy, 8, 136

Ballard, Willis Todhunter, 119-120

Barker, S. Omar, 97, 120-121

Barnes, Charles, 30

Baumhofer, Walter, 130-131

Beadle and Adams, 2

Bedford-Jones, H., 9, 82, 90

Bjorklund, Larry, 27

Boggs, Red, 12

Bond, Lee, 20, 25

Bosworth, Allan R., 21, 28, 59

Bower, Bertha M., 107

Bragg, William F., 21, 24

Brand, Max, *See Faust, Frederick*

Buffalo Bill, 2

Buntline, Ned, *See Judson, Zane Carroll*

Conlon, Ben, *See Gridley, Austin*

Curry, Tom, 40

Bundy, Rex, 83

Burr, John, 27

Carleton, Warren E., 26

Cave, Hugh, 117

Coburn, Walt, 54, 87

Complete Western Book Magazine, 50

Cowboy Movie Thrillers, 51

Cox, Bill, 119

Curry, Tom, 94

David, Don, 40

Davis, Robert H., 80, 85

Deadwood Dick, 3

Delano, Gerry, 53

DeLavy, Edmund J., 131

DeSoto, Raphael, 131

Dime Novels, 1

Dobie, J. Frank, 99

Drago, Harry Sinclair, 50

Dunn, J. Allan, 17

Eggenhoffer, Nick, 131

Elwell, R. Farrington, 132

Evarts, Hal G., 104-105

Faust, Frederick, 7, 11, 54, 57-58, 80, 83, 126

Friend, Oscar J., 42

Gardner, Erle Stanley, 114

Garfield, Brian, 90

Gibney, Al, 115

Gladney, Graves, 74, 132

Glidden, Fred, 7, 54, 89

Grennell, Dean A., 15

Gridley, Austin, 22, 25, 45

Griffin, Andrew A., 24

Gruber, Frank, 4, 58

Harris, R.G., 45

Harrison, C. William, 40

Haycox, Ernest, 82-83

Heckelmann, Charles N., 42

Henderson, George C., 24

Hero Western, 37
Hersey, Harold, 53
Holmes, L.P., 71, 117-118
Hopalong Cassidy, 48, 50
Johnson, W. Ryerson, 45-47, 58
Judson, Zane Carroll, 4, 17
Kelton, Elmer, 70, 96
Krebs, Roland, 120
L'Amour, Louis, 58-59, 70, 93
Leithead, J. Edward, 54, 104
Lemay, Allan, 126
Leonard, Elmore, 71, 115-116
Lone Ranger Magazine, The 42-43
Lowndes, Robert A., 44, 79-80
MacDonald, William Colt, 9, 96,
    125
Masked Rider Western, 42
Maynard, Guy L., 23-24, 39
McCulley, Johnston, 47-48
McLuhan, Marshall, 33
Mix, Tom, 50, 84, 93, 124-125,
    143-144
Movie Western, 51-52
Mulford, Clarence, 48-49, 125
Munsey, Frank, 7, 85
Nafziger, Ray, 41, 53
New York Weekly, 2
Oliphant, Ronald, 17, 23, 27, 62
Olmstead, Harry, 40
Overholser, Wayne D., 105
Patten, Lewis B., 107, 140
Pete Rice Western, 45
Powers, Paul S., 18
Price, E. Hoffman, 12

Raine, William MacLeod, 107
Ranch Romances, 99-100, 121
Rio Kid Western, 40
Rober, Fred, 44
Romance Western, The, 33
Schisgall, Oscar, 42
Scott, H.W., 13, 27, 130
Seth Jones, 2
Shirreffs, Gorden D., 116-117
Shope, Shorty, 131-132
Short, Luke, See Glidden, Fred
Spicy Western Stories, 43-44
Star Western, 40-41
Sturgeon's Law, 141
Thrilling Western, 38, 42
Tilden, Michael, 74
Todd, William A., 24
Tompkins, Walker, 22, 60
True West, 104
Tuttle, W.C., 90-91
Ward, H.J., 43
Wells, Lee, 42
Western Novel and Short Stories, 50
Western Raider, The, 39-40
Western Story Magazine, 3, 7, 9-10,
    45, 48
Western Writers of America, The,
    91, 120
Wheelwright, Thea, 30-31
Wild West Weekly, 12, 39, 44-45
Young Wild West, 2-3, 16
Zane Grey Western, 54-55, 89, 102
Zorro, 47-48, 124-125

PRIVATE EYELASHES

Radio's Lady Detectives

by Jack French

www.privateeyelashes.com

BearManor Media

OLD RADIO. OLD MOVIES. NEW BOOKS.

BearManor Media is a small press publishing Big books. Biographies, script collections, you name it. We love old time radio, voice actors and old films.

Current and upcoming projects include:

The Great Gildersleeve	*Walter Tetley*
The Bickersons Scripts	*Don Ameche*
The Baby Snooks Scripts	*Guy Williams*
Information Please	*Jane Kean*
The Life of Riley	*Joel Rapp*
The Bickersons	*Albert Salmi*
The Ritz Brothers	*Peggy Ann Garner*
Paul Frees	and many more!
Daws Butler	

Write for a free catalog, or visit
http://bearmanormedia.com today.

BearManor Media
P O Box 750
Boalsburg, PA 16827
814-466-7555
info@ritzbros.com